Pit, Pot, and Skillet

PIT·POT·&·SKILLET

Red Caldwell

CORONA PUBLISHING CO.

SAN ANTONIO

1990

Cover design by Donna Jaseckas
Text design by Judi Privett and Alice Evett

ISBN No. 0-931722-81-0
Library of Congress Catalog Card No. 90-80856

Manufactured in the United States of America
90 91 92 93 94   10 9 8 7 6 5 4 3 2 1

For Natha,
whose support and encouragement are the foundations
upon which the final product rests.

ACKNOWLEDGEMENTS

Regardless of what anyone might tell you, *no* book springs from the mind straight to the printer with the author as its only conduit. And *this* one *certainly* didn't!

My bride, Natha, had the unenviable task of translating my handwriting into legible, typed English, as well as the drudgery of proofing numerous drafts prior to submission to the publisher. Since most of the recipes included in this book are the result of trial and error, you can also imagine what many of her suppers were like! It must be hell living in a perpetual test kitchen. Her support and encouragement were critical. Thanks are not enough . . . it's her work as much as mine.

Speaking of trial and error, Tom and Alice Jones of San Marcos, Texas, and Dorothy Wilson of Toronto, Canada, deserve kudos for serving as guinea pigs for many of the recipes included herein. It's a trial being encouraging when you're eating an error.

Charles Kirkham of Dallas comes in for a tip of the black felt for all of his encouragement and enthusiasm for this project.

Alice Evett and David Bowen, editor and publisher respectively, have given new meaning to the word patience, having brought this effort to fruition without once using the words "jerk" or "bozo." Amazing!

Again, Thanks!
Red Caldwell

CONTENTS

INTRODUCTION

Over the years Texans have evolved into an ethnic group all their own, complete with customs, celebrations, and cuisine. It is the last that interests us here. There are those who *must* have a regular 'fix' of barbecue, chili, or chicken-fried steak or they become cranky, irritable, and (*gasp*) unfriendly!

Unfortunately, that which was once commonplace has become scarce. Good scratch chili is hard to find, properly cooked barbecue is an endangered species, and a good chicken-fried steak is extinct in some parts of the state.

What happened? During the last two decades, economic explosion brought countless planeloads of non-Texan types to the state, and traditional Texas-style foods took a back seat to chic. Between fast food, convenience foods, trendy restaurants, and nearly terminal infection of Yuppie Fever, a whole generation forgot to learn how to cook! With the recent economic implosion ". . . the carpetbaggers done packed their bags and went . . .", to quote the song, and the fever was cured by a massive injection of reality. A search for basic values and comforts has taken their place.

When the question "Mom, how do you make meatloaf?" came over the telephone the other day, it struck me that those of us who know how to cook Texas-style have done a lousy job of passing on that experience. What good is knowledge if it's not shared?

I've tried to pass along the atmosphere of Texas Cooking, as well as the "how-to." Most of what's included are the product of trial and error—lots of errors in there, friends. And that's the way you should use the book. If you want to change things up, go for it. There's only two things that can happen, and half of 'em are good!

Since our nearest specialty food store is conveniently located an hour and a half up the Interstate, you'll find that all of the ingredients that we use are readily available at any well-stocked supermarket. Somehow, a three-hour round-trip for a bag of overpriced mushrooms doesn't make a lot of sense. On the other hand, three hours invested in a trip to Fredericksburg for peaches or to Poteet for strawberries is quite logical. Got to get your priorities *straight!*

In some sections, I'll mention a product by brand name. That's not advertising; I've just found that product to be consistently reliable in that particular recipe. Others would probably work just as well, but I function on the theory "if it ain't broke, don't fix it", and haven't tried them. Beer is one exception. While you might change brands, stick with regular brews—no lights, drys, darks, or imports. The Mexican limes referred to are the smaller, golf-ball-size limes. They have more flavor, and they're cheaper than the larger Persian variety. They're also the ones found hanging on your margarita glass at Ma Crosby's—a cultural center just south of the International Bridge in Ciudad Acuña.

Just in case we've used a few terms that are furrin' to you, we've put a Glossary in the back. If you already know what *escabeche* and *posole* mean, never mind.

The reader with a quick eye will observe that this book is long on entree-type foods and short on breads, sweets, and desserts. No mystery there! I don't do my own brain surgery, either.

I hope you enjoy and benefit from this book. If its pages are worn and stained after several years, then I've done my job.

Pit, Pot, and Skillet

Nathan O'Bryant
of Eden, Texas.

Converted refrigerator.

The ubiquitous
barrel barbecue pit.

Chapter One

Stuff You Cook On A Pit

————————— *BARBECUE* —————————

The art of cooking meat with wood smoke

There are basically two types of barbecue—open pit and enclosed pit. Open pit was the first type developed and has been around since they invented dirt. For open pit barbecue, you dig a pit 2–1/2 feet deep, 3-feet wide, and as long as is needed to feed the crowd you invited. Then you fill the pit with wood, start a fire, let it burn down to coals for about ten or twelve hours, put a grill over it, and toss on the meat—basting frequently.

There are several obvious drawbacks to this. Since labor is no longer available for "a dollar a day and found", cutting and hauling 1/2 to 3/4 cord of wood becomes a real chore, and digging the pit truly onerous. A two-foot hole in the ground will strike water in some parts of the country, and a two-inch hole will hit solid rock in others. Urban dwellers will find additional social and legal reasons to reject the open pit. All one needs is to have one's neighbor become "overserved" with a titillating beverage and inadvertently do an impromptu Hindu firewalk while the local fire department is chopping down the privacy fence, hoses in hand! Therefore, we recommend Plan B, the closed pit method.

Closed pit barbecue involves building a fire at one end of an enclosed pit and forcing the smoke to travel the length of the pit to an exit. Somewhere in between, barbecue happens. There are countless pit designs running from huge brick units to various large-diameter pipe fabrications to the ubiquitous 55-gallon drum, various commercial configurations designed for urban dwellers, even the odd converted refrigerator (not a bad cooker, actually).

The type of pit you use is less critical than your willingness to *learn to cook* with it. A recent visitor to my patio summed it up well: "Basically, barbecue is simply stewardship of the fire." How true! I know one guy who won the most prestigious barbecue cook-off in Texas on a #3 washtub. Unfortunately, experience with a given pit is the only true teacher.

To regulate the internal temperature, first you have to know what it is! Many pits have thermometers built in, but for those that don't, a good one can be purchased and installed for $10 to $15. Check around at larger hardware stores. Failing this, an alternative is to use a small internal oven thermometer from a cooking supply store for about $7 to $10.

There should be two air controls on your pit—a draft (on the firebox) and a flue damper, or chimney flap. The draft is the fastest heat control: open it up and the heat increases; shut it down and the heat decreases. The flue damper is used to fine-tune the fire after the draft is set. Never close the damper completely unless you need to knock down a very hot fire quickly, as the pit will cease drawing properly. Over time you'll soon manipulate your pit like a fine old violin.

As to what to burn, there is a wide range of thought on the subject that can lead to large brawls, family feuds, or questions of mental competence. Everybody agrees on what not to burn: pine, cedar, juniper, fir, hackberry, elm, or any other soft, sappy wood. Depending on locale and availability, hardwoods such as oak, mesquite, hickory, pecan, alder, cherry, apple, and peach are favored. My personal favorite is half oak and half mesquite. I like a little pecan, but people get testy when they find you in their pecan grove with a chain saw! Urban cookers can use charcoal with soaked chips and obtain excellent results. If you use a charcoal lighter fluid to ignite the fire, let it burn for 45 minutes before adding meat to clear all the fumes out— unless you *like* the aromatic flavor of naptha!

Regardless of whether your meat choice is brisket or ham, prime rib or goat, pork loin or chicken, always judge your end results on the five basic criteria: tenderness, flavor, tenderness, juiciness, and tenderness. All barbecues should have a good smokey meat flavor, show no signs of dryness, and offer no resistance to being consumed. If it's not tender, nothing else really matters.

As a general rule, remember that the less desirable (i.e., cheaper and tougher) the cut of meat, the longer and slower you should cook it, and the more fat it should contain, proportionately speaking. Although brisket is the only large chunk of beef thoroughly discussed here, the same general principles can be applied to any large (5 pounds plus) chunk of beef—chuck roasts, rump roasts, round roasts, etc. Just figure about an hour per pound at ±220 degrees as a good starting point and go from there. Piece of cake!

There are several ironclad rules of barbecue to get you started:

1. **Never** salt meat prior to cooking. Salt dries and toughens the meat. This includes garlic salt, onion salt, seasoned salt, etc.

2. **Never** use a fork to handle cooking meat. Pierced meat loses juices, causing toughness and dryness. Use tongs or a scoop.

3. **Always** cook meat fat side up. Let gravity natur-
   ally baste and tenderize the meat.
4. **Never** use a sweet and/or tomato basting sauce
   until the last 30 minutes of cooking. The sugar
   caramelizes and burns quickly. Yuck!
5. **Always** preheat the pit and form a bed of coals,
   This saves a lot of misery later.

So with these thoughts in mind, let's crack open a cold one and
go build a fire.

Brisket

Far and away, brisket is the beef cut of choice for lots of
Texas barbecuers. Use 10–11 pound packer-trimmed briskets,
as they are large enough to cook well but small enough to have
a chance of being tender. The larger ones have little hope, and
the smaller ones don't have enough fat (nature's tenderizer).

All briskets have a fat cover on one side. Don't worry about
this—it tells you which side goes up. Turn the brisket over and
press the thick end with your thumbs. Select the brisket that
does not have a large, hard fat-kernel on the thick end. Avoid
value-trimmed, closely-trimmed, or lean-trimmed brisket
pieces—the fat that has been cut off is what creates the tenderness and carries the flavor to an otherwise undistinguished cut
of meat.

COOK AS FOLLOWS:

1. Rub the brisket all over with a seasoning rub (see
   suggestions below)

2. Place meat, fat side up, as far away from the direct heat as possible. Now leave it alone for 12 hours while tending your fire. Try to hold the heat at ±210° in the brisket area. This will take a little trial and error as you learn your pit.

3. After twelve hours, slather on a generous coating of basting sauce (see recipe below). Wrap tightly in aluminum foil, return to pit, and shut the fire down by closing the drafts and damper. Let set in pit for 3–4 hours.

4. Remove the foil, reserving liquid, and let set on cutting board for 20 minutes. Thinly slice across the grain (see diagram), put in serving dish, and pour reserved liquid over the sliced meat.

As a good rule of thumb, you can figure that a brisket will yield about 65% of its original weight. So, a 10-pound brisket serves about 12 normal people (8 ounce serving) or 8 folks who eat like I do!

Serve with Ol' Red's Barbecue Sauce, beans, Natha Lee's Coleslaw, plenty of bread, pickles, onions, jalapeños, and peach cobbler.

Dry Rub #1

Works well on all meat but especially well on brisket and pork.

    1 12-oz. jar Adam's Lemon Pepper Marinade
    1 11-oz. can Gebhardt's chili powder
    4 Tbs. garlic powder (heaping)
    1 Tbs. cayenne pepper

Mix all ingredients together. Shake liberally over meat on all surfaces and rub in well. Store leftovers tightly sealed in refrigerator.

Dry Rub #2

    1/2 cup Real Lemon Juice
    1 11-oz. can Gebhardt's chili powder
    4 Tbs. garlic powder (heaping)
    1 Tbs. cayenne pepper
    2 Tbs. black pepper

Rub meat generously all over with lemon juice. Mix dry ingredients together. Shake liberally over meat on all surfaces and rub in well. Store leftovers tightly sealed in refrigerator.

Dry Rub #3

    1 cup garlic powder
    1 cup black pepper
    1 cup paprika

Mix all ingredients together. Shake liberally over meat on all surfaces and rub in well. Store leftovers tightly sealed in refrigerator.

Basting Sauce

1 lb. butter or margarine
2 onions (peeled and sliced)
5 cloves garlic (crushed)
1 bunch parsley tops (chopped)
1 bottle Lone Star Beer
1 pint cooking oil (not olive, peanut, or safflower)
4 lemons (quartered)
1/2 tsp. cayenne pepper
1/4 cup Worcestershire sauce
2 bay leaves
2 Tbs. chili powder

Melt butter and add onions and garlic. Sauté for 4–5 minutes. Add beer, squeeze in lemon juice, and add rinds. When foam subsides, add all other ingredients and bring to a boil. Reduce to medium-low and simmer for 20 minutes. Keep warm throughout the barbecuing process, adding beer and oil as needed. This is good for any kind of barbecue.

Ol' Red's Barbecue Sauce

2 Tbs. cooking oil
15 cloves garlic (minced)
1/4 cup minced fresh jalapeño peppers

1/4 cup minced fresh serrano peppers
4 cups chopped onions
1 cup Worcestershire sauce
2 cups catsup
1/2 cup cider vinegar
1/2 cup lemon juice
1 cup strong black coffee
2/3 cup brown sugar
6 Tbs. chili powder
1 Tbs. salt
3 Tbs. prepared mustard

Combine onions, garlic, jalapeños, and serranos, with oil. Cook covered over low heat until soft; add everything else, cover, and simmer for 40 minutes. Allow to cool to room temperature and strain into a dish. Process solids in food processor and add to strained liquid, stirring thoroughly. Allow to rest for several hours before serving, to permit flavors to blend. Makes two quarts.

Note: Pass this sauce separately for an excellent addition to your dinner, regardless of which meat you cook. It is not a basting sauce, but a condiment.

Barbecued Ham

1 13- to 19-lb. fresh ham
Rub #3

Preheat pit. Cover surface of ham with rub and place on pit (fat side up) in the coolest part, farthest from direct heat. Hold temperature in area with ham at 210°. Smoke 45 minutes per pound. Remove from heat and let rest for 20 minutes before carving.

Barbecued Ham—Cajun Style

1 13- to 19-lb. fresh ham
8 green cayenne peppers (split lengthwise into quarters)
16 large cloves garlic (peeled and halved)
Rub #3

Preheat pit. With very sharp, thin-blade knife make 32 deep stab incisions into ham. Insert 1/2 clove garlic and 1/4 cayenne into each incision. Cover surface of ham with rub and place on pit (fat side up) in coolest part, farthest from direct heat. Hold temperature in area with ham at 210°. Smoke 45 minutes per pound. Remove from heat and let rest for 20 minutes before carving.

Barbecued Pork Spare Ribs

Two 4-lb. racks of ribs (chine bone removed)
Dry Rub #1
1 qt. Basting Sauce

Preheat pit to 275°. Cover ribs with dry rub and rub in well. Place ribs away from heat sources, directly in path of smoke. Baste and turn ribs every thirty minutes for 3–4 hours or until done. Serve immediately. Serves 6–8.

Barbecued Pork Loin

> One 6- to 8-lb. pork loin
> Dry Rub #1

Preheat pit. Cover meat with dry rub and rub in well. Set meat in middle of indirect heat cooking area, holding the temperature around 250–275°. Cook for about 4 to 5 hours. Remove and allow to rest for 10 minutes before carving.

Note: You can barbecue either whole or boneless pork loins. If you use the boneless version you must watch closely as they cook quite quickly and will fall apart. Cook them less time and in a cooler portion of your pit.

Hint: When serving any of the pork entrees above, you really should consider the Texas Vegetable Medley as a side dish. (See Chapter Two)

Barbecued Chicken

> Two 6- to 7-lb. chickens (I like Sunday Roasters)
> 2 lemons (quartered)
> 2 Tbs. fresh or 1 Tbs. dried rosemary
> 2 medium onions (quartered)
> 1/2 cup cooking oil
> 1 Tbs. black pepper
> 4 cloves garlic
> Black pepper

Preheat pit. Heat together oil, 1 Tbs. black pepper, and 2 crushed garlic cloves for baste. Stuff each bird with 1 lemon, 1 onion, a garlic clove, and half the rosemary. Place into pit at 275—300°, roasting with door closed. Baste with seasoned oil every 20-30 minutes. Cook about 3-1/2 to 4-1/2 hours until the color of a well-worn saddle (a nice medium brown). Remove to cutting board and allow to rest for 15 minutes. Remove stuffing and carve to your pleasure. Serves 8.

Note: You can do halves or quarters in the same manner. Obviously you can't stuff 'em but you baste 'em with seasoned oil 20-30 minutes and turn 'em once. A full pit of quarters takes about 2 to 2-1/2 hours.

Hint: Watch the grocery stores sales. They'll run hindquarters on sale *cheap* for 10-lb. bags. Dinner for 8 for less than 5 bucks!

After whole birds are quartered, freeze the quarters in serving-size portions. Thaw out later and serve at room temperature with fresh fruit, cheese, a loaf of crusty bread, and white wine for a quickie dinner that beats the regular frozen kind.

Smoked Turkey

One 12- to 14-lb. self-basting turkey
2 ribs celery (quartered)
2 onions (halved)
2 cloves garlic (crushed)
Black pepper
3/4 cup cooking oil
2 cloves garlic
1 Tbs. black pepper

Preheat pit. Heat together oil, 1 Tbs. black pepper, and 2 crushed garlic cloves for baste. Rinse turkey inside and out, reserving neck and giblets. Stuff with celery, onions, and garlic. Sprinkle outside of bird with black pepper. Place on pit away from direct heat and as far as possible from heat source. Cook at ±200° for 18 hours basting occasionally to protect skin. Remove to a cutting board and let rest for 30 minutes before carving.

Note: If you are cooking a roast or brisket at the same time, put the roast on the shelf *above* the turkey and dripping fat will baste the bird for you!

Hint: A good "do-ahead" for a party, particularly at Christmas. Cook the bird a week ahead, carve and freeze. On Party Day, thaw and serve at room temperature as the central part of a sandwich tray.

Barbecued Quail

8 quail (dressed)
4 fresh jalapeños (stemmed, seeded, and halved
  lengthwise)
4 cloves garlic (halved)
8 small onion wedges
8 strips bacon

Preheat pit. Stuff each quail with 1/2 jalapeño, 1/2 clove garlic, and 1 onion wedge. Wrap each quail lengthwise with a strip of bacon. Roast in indirect hot smoke for 45 minutes to 1-1/4 hours until done. Remove and reserve bacon, discard stuffing, and halve birds. Serves 4.

Note: Have some flavored oil (see recipe for smoked turkey) handy in case birds start to dry out. Watch these little fellows closely for they can turn into charcoal very quickly.

Barbecued Salmon

Some friends of ours from Seattle, Bob and Dixie Whitefield, showed us how the Washington folks barbecue their salmon. The original recipe called for lemons instead of limes, and parsley instead of cilantro. However, the recipe also called for alder, the wood of choice in the Pacific Northwest. We've been fresh out of alder for a couple of eons, if we every had any to start out with, so I substituted straight mesquite, the national tree of South Texas, and the other two substitutions were made because they sounded good with mesquite.

> One 3–5 pound boneless side of salmon (skin on)
> 1 lb. butter (not margarine this time please)
> 8 cloves garlic (crushed)
> 2 medium onions (peeled, thinly sliced, and separated into rings)
> 4 small limes (thinly sliced)
> 2 oranges (thinly sliced)
> 1 Tbs. cilantro (minced)
> Black pepper

Preheat pit. Form a boat or pan out of heavy aluminium foil with 1–1/2 inch sides, large enough to hold the salmon. Melt butter in small saucepan, add garlic, and turn off burner. Place boat in pit close to heat source but not over direct heat. Put salmon in boat, skin side down. Sprinkle with black pepper and scatter onion, orange, lime, and cilantro over fish. Then pour garlic butter over salmon. Close cooker and smoke for approximately 7 minutes. Using a long spoon, baste salmon with butter from boat, and every 5–8 minutes thereafter to prevent drying. When fish flakes it's done (approximately 45 minutes). Serves 6–8.

Fajitas

A lot of good meat has been wrecked in the 10 years since fajitas were "discovered." The whole idea was to make good use of chewy cuts of beef. Sirloin is *not* improved by this procedure. And "chicken fajitas" is a contradiction in terms.

2–3 lbs. beef skirt (untrimmed, untenderized)
One 8-oz. bottle herbs and garlic oil-based salad dressing
1 Lone Star Beer
3 Tbs. chili powder
1-1/2 tsp. garlic powder
2 Tbs. Adam's Lemon Pepper Marinade
3–4 small Mexican limes (juiced)
2 tsp. cumin
1 large onion (minced)
2 Tbs. minced cilantro
1 Tbs. Worcestershire sauce
1 tsp. cayenne pepper
1 bay leaf

Preheat pit. Mix all ingredients except beef together to make a marinade. Pour over meat in a non-reactive container. Cover and stir occasionally for 6–8 hours prior to cooking. Cook in either of these ways:

A. If you have the space, smoke the fajitas for about 30 minutes with pure mesquite smoke, then cook over direct heat (mesquite coals are best) for about 4–7 minutes per side. Baste with marinade while cooking.

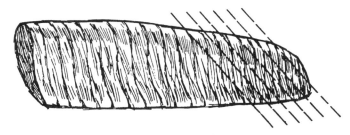

B. Cook over direct heat (mesquite coals are best) for 6–10 minutes per side depending on how done you like your meat. Baste with marinade while cooking.

Immediately slice meat (see illustrations and instructions— very important). Serve with guacamole and *pico de gallo* in warm flour tortillas. Figure 1/2 lb. of meat and 3–4 flour tortillas per person.

Note: For large groups of 12 or more, a non-Styrofoam beer cooler is a great marinade bucket.

How to slice fajitas: (see illustration) The meat will be a lot more tender if you will cut it at a 45-degree angle to its "grain" and hold your knife at a 45-degree angle.

Barbecued Cabrito (Goat)

2 hindquarters of kid (goat), 4–5 lbs. each
Dry Rub #1
2 quarts basting sauce

Preheat pit to 275°. Cover cabrito with dry rub and rub it in well. Place in pit away from heat sources, directly in path of smoke. Baste and turn every thirty minutes for 3–4 hours or until done. Serve immediately.

Note: Cabrito is quite lean, so it has to be watched carefully and basted often. Usually I'll just smoke it for 1–2 hours, basting frequently, then wrap it in foil to finish up the cooking process. Otherwise it gets too dry. Only use the hindquarter, since there ain't enough meat in the forequarter to make a tamale.

A word of warning: The last few times I went looking for cabrito, it was hard to find and expensive for the amount of use-able meat!

— ABOUT SMOKE ROASTING —

Smoke roasting, for lack of a better term, simply means using the pit in place of a conventional oven. After all, a convection oven cooks with hot forced air, so why not smoke? I came up with this idea a couple of hours before dinner guests arrived one evening, and immediately *after* our conventional oven croaked.

You must be able to hold the temperature close to 325° in order to achieve the desired results, but practice makes perfect. Also, cooking time is much shorter than with conventional barbecue. Using a meat thermometer is a must!

Prime Rib

A true prime rib still has the bones on it. Being lazy, I use the boneless ribeye (same meat, no bones). If yours has the bones, just rely on your meat thermometer.

One 4-1/2 lb. boneless ribeye, small end, flap on
1/4 small cabbage, quartered
2 medium onions, quartered
2 garlic cloves, peeled
2 carrots, quartered
1 turnip, quartered
1/2 bunch parsley, tops only
5 cans consommé
Black pepper
Disposable roasting pan large enough to hold prime rib

Preheat pit to 325°. Mix veggies together and spread in an even layer in the roasting pan. Sprinkle meat with black pepper and place on top of veggies. Roast in closed pit for approximately 30 minutes. Pour all 5 cans consommé over roast, close pit, and continue to roast until meat thermometer reads 135° for rare. Remove to a cutting board, tent with foil, and allow to stand for 15–20 minutes. Slice into 4 servings. Strain liquid left in bottom of roasting pan to use for gravy. 4 large servings.

Note: This is wonderful with steamed spinach with lime butter, green salad with blue cheese dressing, and a full-bodied red wine.

Leftover suggestions: Store in gravy until ready to reheat in microwave. It makes the basis for a great brunch or a Sunday night sandwich.

Rack of Lamb

2 racks lamb (2-1/2 lbs. each, chine bone removed)
Black pepper

Garlic powder
Olive oil

Preheat pit. Rub meat with olive oil, and sprinkle with black pepper and garlic powder. Place both pieces, meaty side up, in a disposable roasting pan. Place in pit, close door, and roast at 325° until an internal temperature of 150° is reached—about 1-1/2 hours. Remove to carving board, let rest for 15 minutes, and carve. Serves 4.

Suggestions: While it might be a cliché, steamed fresh asparagus and parsleyed new potatoes are still way out in front of whatever is in second place as side dishes.

Note: Bearnaise sauce is wonderful with mesquite-smoked lamb. Another suggestion is to try jalapeño jelly instead of the old standby, mint jelly.

Smoked Country Ribs with Hill Country Peach Sauce

8 country pork ribs about 3/4 inch thick
1/4 cup lemon juice
Black pepper

Rub lemon juice into both sides of ribs. Sprinkle with pepper. Place ribs in indirect heat, about 250° for 2 to 2-1/2 hours, turning once until done. Serve with peach sauce.

FOR THE SAUCE:

2-1/2 cups fresh peaches, pitted, peeled, and sliced
1/3 cup brown sugar, packed
1 fresh jalapeño, stemmed and minced
1 cup water
2 Tbs. fresh lime juice
1 Tbs. minced fresh cilantro

Combine peaches, sugar, water, and jalapeño in a medium saucepan. Simmer over moderate heat for twenty minutes. Allow to cool to room temperature. Puree in food processor and stir in lime juice and cilantro just before serving.

Barbecued Veggies

8 yellow squash (sliced to 3/4-inch thick)
6 medium zucchini (sliced to about 1/2-inch thick)
3 large sweet onions, thinly sliced (Texas 1015 are best)
3-4 large tomatoes (cut into eighths)
1 stick butter or margarine (melted)

Mix all veggies together. Place on a large sheet of aluminum foil and pour butter over them. Seal in the foil and place in closed pit for 1-1/2 hours. Serves 8.

Foiled Bananas

4 bananas (peeled and halved lengthwise)
1/2 stick butter (melted)
2 tsp. brown sugar

Stir brown sugar into melted butter. Place bananas on a large piece of aluminum foil, closely packed. Pour butter mixture over bananas and seal foil to make a pouch. Place in coolest part of pit for 20–30 minutes. Serves 4.

Note: These are not Bananas Foster but are quick, easy, and go well with homemade ice cream.

Baked Onions

>   4 large sweet onions
>   1-1/2 sticks unsalted butter at room temperature

Peel onions and core from stem end using apple corer. Discard core. Fill holes with butter and wrap each onion individually in foil. Place on pit at medium heat for 1–1/2 hours until cooked through. Serves 8.

Note: Works well with apples, too.

Smokey Mushrooms

These little jewels are so quick and easy, you ought to be ashamed to take the compliments you're gonna get!

>   1 stick butter at room temperature (margarine works fine)
>   3 large green onions, finely chopped (including tops)
>   3 large cloves garlic, peeled and crushed through a press
>   1 8-oz. pkg. mushrooms, rinsed and stemmed

Combine butter, garlic, and green onions thoroughly. Stuff each mushroom cap with butter combination. Place in a shallow roasting pan, stuffed side up. Place in the hotter portion of your pit for about five to ten minutes until butter has melted and the mushrooms have begun to give up their juice. Serve immediately, while waiting for the Prime Rib, Rack of Lamb, or whatever. Serves about 4. Any leftover butter can be used to spread on the bread that you ought to be getting ready for the main course.

GRILLING

Grilling, as opposed to barbecue, requires cooking over direct heat, and at a much higher heat. Too often, steaks and chops grilled at home fail to produce the desired results either because the fire wasn't hot enough and/or the meat was left on the fire for too long a time for its thickness, or both.

The most common fuel for grilling is charcoal, so we'll start with the charcoal fire. Begin by arranging the charcoal in a mound, and dosing the mound well with charcoal starting fluid. Ignite and let burn down until most of the outer briquets are covered with gray ash. Scatter the briquets until they form a uniform single-layered bed, with the coals just barely separated from one another. Immediately, place prepared meat on grill. Sear for two minutes. (Time will depend upon thickness of meat; more about that later.) Turn meat and cook for 3 to 6 minutes, turn again for an additional 2 to 4 minutes until desired doneness is reached. Keep a filled water pistol handy in case of bad flare-ups, but minor grease flares should be ignored.

Selecting meat for the grill: Steaks and chops over one inch thick do best. About 1-1/4 inch to 1-1/2 inch is ideal. Thinner cuts must be watched closely and turned more frequently or "early charcoal" will result. Thick steaks with a heavy bone— T-bones, porterhouses, or full-cut sirloins—require a little lower heat level, since the meat nearest the bone will require a little longer cooking time.

Some Pointers:

1. **Never** use a fork to turn meat; same as in barbequing, the juices will run out leaving dry, tough meat. Invest in a good set of long-handled tongs. Long tongs save wear and tear on the hands when reaching across the fire, and serve a variety of other uses, like handling baked potatoes and corn on the cob.

2. **Never** salt meat before cooking. It causes the meat to dry out and toughen.

3. **On thinner cuts of meat**, especially, use a butter or oil baste to prevent drying (particularly on chicken breasts and shellfish) and cook quickly.

Steaks:

Sprinkle black pepper and garlic powder on both sides twenty minutes before cooking or sprinkle lemon pepper marinade and chili powder on both sides before cooking. Or baste while cooking with lemon garlic butter, lime onion butter, or soy sauce and ginger butter.

- Lemon Garlic Butter: Melt one stick butter, add juice of one lemon and 1/2 tsp. garlic powder. Baste on every side and spread over cooked steaks when they are served.

- Lime Onion Butter: Melt one stick butter, add juice of 1-1/2 small limes, 1/2 tsp. garlic powder, 1/2 onion (minced). Baste on each side and serve over cooked steak.
- Soy Sauce Butter: Melt one stick butter, add 1 Tbs. grated fresh ginger, and 2 Tbs. soy sauce. Baste on each side and serve over cooked meat.

Chicken Breasts or Hindquarters:

Use an oil/butter base marinade and baste to keep these delicate parts from drying. Cook them quickly over high heat to sear, then move to cooler section of the grill to complete the cooking process. Soak the breasts for an hour before cooking. A good example of a marinade baste is:

> 1 cup cooking oil
> 2 Tbs. chopped fresh rosemary
> 2 cloves garlic (peeled and crushed)
> 1 Tbs. lemon juice
> 1 Tbs. black pepper

Want it real simple?

> One 8-oz. bottle Italian dressing (oil base, not cream base)
> 2 tsp. crushed red pepper flakes
> Juice of one lemon

Pork Steaks or Chops:

Rub with lemon juice, sprinkle with black pepper. Meat 1 inch or thicker works best. Cook like you would steaks.

Lamb Chops:

Amazing that most folks have little or no experience cooking lamb although Texas is the largest sheep-producing state in the nation. Oh well, that leaves more for us, doesn't it? Use chops 1-1/4 to 1-1/2 inch thick. Rub with olive oil, lime juice, and black pepper. Cook as with steaks. Garnish with jalapeño jelly.

Leg of Lamb:

Have your butcher bone and butterfly the 4-5 lb. leg. Rub all over with olive oil, black pepper, and fresh oregano. Allow to set one hour with this rub before cooking. Sear bone side down for 3-4 minutes, turn for 3-4 minutes, basting with oil. Continue in this manner until meat is medium (about 6-7 minutes per side). Garnish with jalapeño jelly.

Quick Marinade for Grilled Chicken or Pork

1/4 cup soy sauce
1 Tbs. prepared mustard
1 tsp. brown sugar

Combine all ingredients thoroughly and spread over both sides of four chicken breasts or pork chops. Allow to marinate at room temperature for an hour. Grill over medium coals for 3-4 minutes per side.

Shish Kabobs

3 lbs. sirloin, cut into 1-1/2 inch cubes
8-12 large mushroom caps, soaked in oil from can of jalapeños
2 large bell peppers, stemmed, cored, and cut in eighths

2 large sweet onions, quartered
Marinade (see below)

Marinate steak for 2 hours before cooking. On 4 skewers, alternate sirloin, onion, and bell pepper pieces until skewers are loaded. Thread mushrooms on a separate skewer. Wash your hands after this! Grill over medium coals for 3 minutes, turn 180°, and repeat until all 4 sides are cooked, basting with every turn. Put mushrooms on grill for the last five minutes, turning twice. Baste everything with the jalapeño *escabeche* once. Serve on rice cooked with beef broth. Serves 4–6.

Marinade:

1 Lone Star Beer
One 6-oz. bottle soy sauce
2 Tbs. fresh grated ginger
4 cloves garlic (crushed through a press)

Mix together and pour over meat. Add 1/3 cup oil to remaining marinade after constructing shish kabobs and use for a baste.

Rio Grande Catfish

4 8-oz. catfish filets (skinless and boneless)
2 fresh jalapeños, stemmed and minced
3 fresh serranos, stemmed and minced
1/2 medium onion, diced
2 cloves garlic, crushed through a press
1 cup cooking oil
1/2 cup freshly squeezed lime juice
1/2 Tbs. comino

2 Tbs. cilantro leaves, minced
1 cup tomatoes, peeled, diced and chilled

Combine everything but the tomatoes and catfish in a blender and spin to mix. Place the filets in a nonreactive container large enough to hold them in a single layer. Pour the marinade over the filets and cover. Turn the filets *once* after thirty minutes. After a total marinating time of no more than one hour, cook quickly over very hot mesquite coals, about 2–4 minutes per side, basting with the marinade. Place each filet on a plate and top with 1/4 cup of the chilled tomatoes. Serves 4.

Barbecued Shrimp

Be careful. Shrimp must cook very quickly over very hot coals. Shrimp that overcook are quite tough.

32 large shrimp, deheaded but not peeled
1/2 cup bottled Italian dressing
2 Tbs. Worcestershire sauce
2 Mexican limes, juiced
1 Tbs. minced cilantro
1/2 tsp. cumin
1/2 onion, minced

Preheat pit. Combine all ingredients except shrimp. Put shrimp into large sealable plastic bag with marinade. Refrigerate for 2–3 hours, turning the bag occasionally. Skewer 8 shrimps, head to tail, on each of four skewers. Grill over very hot coals for 2–3 minutes maximum, turn and baste with marinade. Cook additional 2 minutes. Serves 4.

Easy Anticuchos

1 lb. beef tenderloin cut into 1-inch cubes
Juice from 1 qt. can jalapeños in *escabeche*

Place meat in a non-reactive bowl. Pour *escabeche* over meat and toss. Allow to rest for an hour. Skewer chunks of meat on 4 soaked wooden skewers. Grill over hot coals for 1–1/2 to 2 minutes per side, basting with marinade. Makes 4 appetizer servings.

Alternate idea: Skewer 2 chunks on small soaked skewers. Grill as above and serve as snacks at an outdoor cocktail party.

Colorful Grilled Corn

1 10-oz. pkg. frozen corn
2 large green onions, finely sliced with their tops
1/2 large sweet red bell pepper
1/2 stick butter
Black pepper to taste

In a medium bowl, break up the frozen corn kernels. Add the onions and diced bell pepper. Place corn mixture on a sheet of aluminum foil and top with the butter which has been cut in thin pats. Sprinkle with pepper and seal foil into a pouch. Cook in a hot pit for 30–45 minutes. Serves 4.

The Ultimate Jalapeño Burger

Eight 1/4-lb. lean hamburger patties
4 slices Monterey Jack cheese
4 slices American cheese
Nacho jalapeño slices
Grilled onions

Preheat grill with medium bed of coals. Place 4 hamburger patties on work surface. Top each with a slice of Monterey Jack cheese, 1 Tbs. each of grilled onions and jalapeño slices, and a slice of American cheese. Top with another hamburger pattie and seal the edges. Cook for 5 minutes per side over medium coals. Serve on warmed buns with your choice of dressings and goodies.

Note: While not mandatory, cold beer is strongly recommended for the beverage with this burger.

Meal in a Pouch

Before there was dehy camp food, boily bags, or RV's, there was a wholesome meal in a pouch. It has fed generations of Scouts and is well worth remembering for an all-day outing.

Combine the following on aluminium foil squares. Per serving:

1/2 lb. lean ground meat mixed with 1 tsp. Worcestershire sauce, 1/4 tsp. garlic powder, and salt and pepper to taste.

1 thick onion slice
1 thick bell pepper slice
1 medium potato, peeled and cut into eighths

Make two patties per pouch. On top of first pattie add the onion and bell pepper, top with second pattie and seal edges. Arrange potatoes around pattie. Seal foil pouch and cook over low coals for 45 minutes to 1-1/4 hours until done.

Chapter Two
Stuff You Cook In A Pot

L ong simmering and slow cooking seem to have gone the way of two-bit beer and the dodo bird. However, that's the only way to evoke the harmony of flavors that your spirit craves. It's also the best way to prepare a variety of foods deemed untrendy (pronounced cheap!). Ranch and trail cooks—and grandmothers, too—knew all about this. You don't think they just used the middle third of the steer or only the breast of the chicken, do you? Obviously, the time constraints of the modern world and the two-wage-earner family restrict you somewhat, but *rejoice!* for many of the following recipes freeze beautifully. So, you can cook one or more of these on Sunday, freeze 'em, and eat like normal people later in the week.

I use the term "Dutch oven" a lot. Usually, this conjures up a vision of cast iron, but there are non-stick-coated heavy aluminum, enamel-coated cast iron, and heavy stainless steel that all do just as well. What you should have is heavy material (to hold the heat) and a good fitting lid. Something in the 5 to 7 quart area is just right. (A word of warning about cast iron — tomatoes react with cast iron to produce a very metallic taste, so plan accordingly. The same can be said for uncoated aluminum.)

If you don't already have one, give serious thought to non-stick-coated heavy aluminum. They're very forgiving about scorching, and they clean up quickly (no small point). However, *everybody* ought to own a *well-seasoned* cast iron Dutch oven as well. They make a thoughtful wedding present. By the time the cook is seasoned, the pot'll be seasoned, too!

——— *SOUPS AND GUMBOS* ———

Beef Broth

Usually, you'll run into broth-making in continental cookbooks, and it's touted as something special. This is not the case. Homemade broth is extremely easy to make and store, and, like fresh herbs, will ruin you for the canned variety. The two basic requirements are a pot of sufficient size, and time.

If you don't already have a 12–16 quart pot (What? You don't?), now is the time to make the investment. Choose well and buy to last a lifetime!

> 4–5 lbs. sliced beef neck bones (or more)
> 3 onions, sliced

Preheat broiler. Spread onions over a shallow roasting pan and place meat chunks in a single layer on top of onions. Place in broiler. When meat is quite brown, turn it and repeat until it is browned on both sides. Dump onions, meat, and pan juices into a stockpot or kettle (12–16 quart). Add 8 quarts of water, bring to a boil, reduce heat to simmer and cook uncovered for 6–8 hours, skimming occasionally. Strain into container and allow to cool. Freeze in pint containers.

To make a truly concentrated broth, boil 1 quart of strained broth until reduced to 2-1/2 or 3 cups.

Broth and stocks are the basis of homemade soups, stews, and chilis. So make lots; it doesn't take any longer.

Chicken Broth

We don't have a recipe for chicken broth. Every time we toss a couple of fat cluckers into the pot, we get halfway to broth, say "What the heck?" and have chicken and dumplings instead (see recipe elsewhere in this chapter).

Roux

Instrumental to making gumbos, roux can be used in a variety of dishes as a thickener and/or flavoring.

    1 cup flour
    1 cup oil

In a large skillet, combine flour and oil over medium low heat. Stir frequently at first, and constantly towards the end. About 45 minutes to 1 hour is about right for a rich, dark brown roux.

Don't try to hurry this process by cooking the roux too hot—it burns *every* time. Burned roux is foul tasting and a pain to clean up.

Beef Gumbo

2-3 lbs. lean beef (round, sirloin, rump, trimmed chuck) cut
    into 1/4- by 1- by 3-inch strips
1 cup red wine
1 Tbs. black pepper
2 bay leaves
6 Tbs. oil
2 large onions, peeled and chopped
3 cloves garlic, peeled and minced
2 large fresh green cayenne peppers (or jalapeños and ser-
    ranos if no cayennes are available) stemmed and
    chopped
4-5 green onions with tops, chopped fine
1/4 cup flour
2 qts. or 4 cans beef broth
1 cup chopped parsley
1/2 Tbs. thyme
2 cups tomatoes, peeled, seeded, and chopped
1 recipe roux
Salt and pepper to taste
Tabasco sauce to taste

Combine wine, black pepper, and 1 bay leaf. Pour over meat
in a non-reactive bowl. Toss and set aside for an hour. In a large
Dutch oven combine 3 Tbs. oil, onions, garlic, peppers, and green
onions. Sauté until softened. Drain meat and dust in 1/4 cup
flour. Brown in a skillet in 3 Tbs. oil. Drain and add to Dutch
oven. Add beef broth, and water to cover if needed. Simmer
covered for 1/2 hour. Add parsley, 1 bay leaf, thyme, and tomatoes, and simmer for another 30 minutes. Add roux and simmer

for another hour. Serve over rice or noodles. Pass filé gumbo and Tabasco.

Corn Chowder

My wife, Natha, brought this recipe to the marriage. It is a winter favorite.

1/2 lb. thick sliced bacon, diced
1 medium onion, coarsely chopped
3 ribs celery, coarsely chopped
2 Tbs. flour
4 cups milk
1 can cream-style corn
3–4 potatoes, peeled and cubed
Fresh parsley, snipped
Salt and pepper to taste

Boil potatoes in covered saucepan until tender. Sauté bacon until crisp in Dutch oven, remove and drain, reserving 3 Tbs. drippings. Add onions and celery to drippings, cook until onion is tender (celery will still be crisp). Blend in flour and cook until mixture is bubbly. Remove from heat and stir in milk. Heat until boiling, stirring constantly, until slightly thickened. Stir in corn, potatoes, salt and pepper to taste. Heat thoroughly. Garnish with bacon and parsley. Serves 6.

Note: You may substitute the potato water for a portion of the milk to make a thinner soup.

Chicken Gumbo

Being a "white meat" person, I make this with chicken breasts, but you can use whatever you like.

6 chicken breasts on the bone
1 large onion, peeled and chopped
1 bunch green onions with tops, thinly sliced
1 bell pepper, diced
4 ribs celery, diced
3 Tbs. oil
2 qts. or 4 cans chicken broth
1 cup chopped parsley leaves
1 cup tomatoes, peeled and chopped
1/2 tsp. cayenne pepper
1-1/2 tsp. black pepper
1 recipe roux

Sauté onion, green onion, bell pepper, and celery in a Dutch oven. Add chicken breasts, broth, parsley, and tomatoes, with water to cover, and simmer for 45 minutes. Add cayenne, black pepper, and roux. Simmer for 1 hour. Serve over rice. Pass Tabasco and filé gumbo at table.

Bubba's Leek and Potato Soup

1–1/2 sticks butter
3 large leeks
2 medium onions
1 qt. half-and-half

Velveeta cheese
1 clove garlic
5 large white potatoes
Salt and white pepper to taste

Dice potatoes and boil until well done. Drain most of the water off. Chop leek and onion very fine and sauté in butter with finely minced garlic. Combine with cooked potatoes. Add half-and-half to make soup mixture as desired. Simmer until done, stirring often to prevent scorching. Add cheese, salt, and white pepper to taste; cook until cheese is melted.

Note: The amount of cheese will vary with taste. Start with 1/2 cup and work up or down from there. We use about 3/4 cup.

Courtesy of "Bubba" Reinke, San Marcos, Texas

Larrideaux's Shrimp and Okra Gumbo

1/4 cup oil
1/4 cup flour
2 large onions, chopped
3 Tbs. butter
4 cups okra, coarsely chopped
2-2/3 cups tomatoes, chopped and seeded
2 large green peppers, seeded and chopped
4 large garlic cloves, minced
2 Tbs. butter
2-1/2 pounds medium shrimp, shelled, deveined (reserve
      heads and tails)
2-1/2 quarts boiling stock (see recipe)
2 chicken bouillon cubes

2 Tbs. crushed dried red peppers
4 tsp. salt
2 bay leaves
2 tsp. Worcestershire sauce
1 tsp. ground allspice
1/2 tsp. freshly ground black pepper
1/4 tsp. dried thyme leaves
2 Tbs. filé powder
Hot cooked rice
Tabasco sauce

Mix oil and flour in a small heavy saucepan; cook over low heat, stirring frequently, until the roux is a dark mahogany color—about 45 minutes. Roux must get very dark brown but not burned; do not under cook. Reserve. Sauté onions in 3 Tbs. butter in large heavy Dutch oven until soft—about five minutes. Stir in okra. Sauté until okra is tender—about 3 minutes. Stir in tomatoes; sauté 30 minutes. Sauté green peppers and garlic in 2 Tbs. butter in large skillet 5 minutes. Add shrimps. Sauté until shrimps turn pink—about 5 minutes. Place heads and shells in approximately 4 quarts of water and boil for 1 hour. Strain mixture and use the stock (2-1/2 qts.) in the next step. Add the shrimp mixture, stock bouillon, red peppers, salt, bay leaves, Worcestershire, allspice, black pepper, thyme, and reserved roux to the okra mixture. Simmer covered 1-1/2 hours.

Remove from heat; let stand 10 minutes. (If gumbo is too hot when filé powder is added, it will become stringy and inedible.) Stir in 2 Tbs. filé powder. Ladle into serving bowls; top each with a scoop of rice. Pass the filé powder and Tabasco sauce. The slow cooking produces the distinctive blending of flavors that some gumbo eaters claim achieves perfection on the second day. Gumbo to be reheated the second day should not have filé added until it is served. **Laissez les bons temps rouler!**

Compliments of Larry Burruss, San Marcos, Texas

Onion Soup

> 1-1/2 qts. beef broth
> 3 cups concentrated beef broth
> 3 large onions, peeled, halved through stem end, and thinly sliced
> 3 Tbs. minced parsley
> 1 clove garlic, peeled, and crushed through a press
> 2 Tbs. unsalted butter
> 1-1/2 oz. dry sherry
> 2 tsp. soy sauce
> Parmesan cheese

Melt butter in 4-quart pot. Add garlic and onions, cover and reduce heat to low, and cook 5–10 minutes until onions are soft. Add all beef broth and simmer covered for 30 minutes. Add parsley, soy sauce, and sherry, and simmer for 15 minutes. After soup is in the bowl, sprinkle generously with Parmesan cheese. Serves 6.

Split Pea Soup

> 2 lbs. dried split peas
> 1 lb. ham—preferably on a bone, but it has to be *ham*

2 medium onions, peeled and sliced
1 tsp. garlic powder
Black pepper and salt to taste
Milk

Rinse peas and cover with cold water to soak overnight. Drain. In a decent-sized pot (5 quarts or so), cover with water, add ham, onion, and garlic powder. Bring to a boil, reduce to a very slow boil, uncovered, and cook until peas have disintegrated—about 3–4 hours. Add a little water as needed, but be careful towards the end as the soup will want to stick. Add milk (or cream, or half-and-half) to desired consistency. Season with salt and pepper. Serve with good dark bread with hot mustard for the bread. Suggested beverage: cold beer. This is a meal in itself.

Turkey Soup

After you've demolished that lovely roasted turkey and sliced off the leftovers for sandwiches, don't toss out the carcass and trimmings. It's soup time! You can make the broth while you're recovering from dinner.

Turkey carcass, bones, wings, wing tips, etc.
3 ribs celery, chunked
2–3 carrots, chunked
2 onions, peeled and halved
3 large parsley sprigs
Fresh black pepper, to taste

Place carcass, celery, carrots, onions, parsley, and pepper in a large stock pot. Cover with water, bring to a boil, reduce heat and simmer uncovered for 7–8 hours, skimming occasionally. Strain broth, discarding vegetables and bones, but reserving meat. Freeze in quart containers.

TO MAKE SOUP: Reheat two quarts of broth (with meat) to a boil. Add 1 Tbs. soy sauce, 1–1/2 oz. dry sherry, and 1 tsp. garlic powder. Add 1 to 2 cups fresh noodles and cook until noodles are al dente. Serves 4.

Vegetable Soup

> 3 quarts beef broth, preferably homemade
> 1 lb. carrots, scraped, peeled, and sliced
> 2–4 ribs celery, thin sliced
> 2 medium onions, peeled and chopped
> 2 cloves garlic, minced
> 2 lbs. potatoes, peeled and cubed
> 2 Tbs. butter
> 2 bay leaves
> 1 tsp. thyme
> 1/2 tsp. oregano
> One 10-oz. package frozen peas
> One turnip, finely diced
> Salt and pepper to taste
> 1/4 cup red wine (optional)

If using homemade broth, bone out the meat from the broth-making process and add the meat to the pot of soup, discarding the bones. Melt butter over medium heat and add onions and garlic. When the onions start to soften, add the broth, meat,

carrots, celery, bay leaf, thyme, oregano, wine, and turnips. Bring
to a boil. Reduce to simmer and cook for 45 minutes. Add potatoes and simmer for 20 minutes. Add peas and cook for 20 more
minutes. Salt and pepper to taste. Makes about 4 quarts. Make
this a day ahead, refrigerate, and reheat when ready to eat. The
flavors really blend then!

STEWS

Red's Real Beef Stew

> 3 lbs. beef stew meat (lean chuck is ideal) trimmed of fat
> and cut into 1 to 1-1/2 inch chunks
> 3/4 cup flour
> 3 tsp. black pepper
> Oil for skillet
> 3 qts. beef stock (see recipe) or canned beef broth
> 2/3 cup red burgundy (*cheap* non-vintage)
> 1 onion, peeled and quartered
> 6 cloves garlic, crushed
> 3 bay leaves
> 1-1/2 cups chopped celery tops
> 1 bunch parsley tops, chopped
> 2 tsp. thyme
> 1 lb. carrots, peeled and cut into 1 inch chunks
> 2 large turnips, peeled and cut into 1 inch chunks
> 1 cup thinly sliced celery
> 2-3 large onions, peeled and chopped
> 1/4 head cabbage, chopped
> 3 lbs. potatoes, cubed (peeling is optional—I don't)
> 1/2 cup red burgundy (same stuff as before)

1 recipe roux
1 Tbs. Worcestershire sauce

Mix the flour and 2 tsp. pepper in a paper bag and shake meat
in bag to coat. Brown meat in pan with enough oil to cover the
bottom. Repeat until all meat is browned. When browned, add
meat to a large (10–12 qt.) pot. Add beef stock, 2/3 cup wine,
onion, garlic, bay leaves, celery tops, 1 bunch parsley, and 2 tsp.
thyme. Bring to a boil, reduce to simmer (covered), and cook
until meat starts to become tender—about 1-1/2 hours. Add
a little water as needed. Add carrots, turnips, celery, onions, cabbage, 1 tsp. thyme, 1 tsp. black pepper, Worcestershire, and 1/2
cup wine. Continue cooking for 30 minutes. Keep adding water
as needed. Add potatoes, rest of parsley, and continue cooking
(covered) until potatoes are done. Add roux, reduce heat, and
simmer slowly for 45 minutes. (If you don't want to go to the
trouble of making a roux, finely grate 1-1/2 cups of potatoes
and add to pot when you put in the beef stock.)

Serves a bunch. This is the kind of pot that you make, dine
upon, take for lunch the next day, and freeze for quickie dinners
later. Serve with a good Beaujolais, green salad, and lots of crusty
bread. For those who are no longer pretentious, peach cobbler
with Lazy Man's Ice Cream (see Finishers) makes a decent
dessert.

Cheap Chicken Stew

When the grocery store runs a special on 10-pound bags
of chicken hindquarters. stock up. This recipe arose from not
being able to pass up a bargain!

6 lbs. chicken hindquarters (about 9 or 10), rinsed and drained
4 ribs celery, with tops, chopped
3 large onions, peeled and chopped
1/2 cup chopped parsley
4 cans chicken broth
4–5 cloves garlic, minced
4 Tbs. fresh rosemary
1 bunch parsley tops, chopped
2 lbs. potatoes, peeled and chunked
1-1/2 oz. dry sherry
1 Tbs. soy sauce
Salt and pepper to taste

Put first seven ingredients in a large pot, add water to cover. Bring to a boil, reduce heat and simmer uncovered. Cook for 4 or 5 hours, stirring, skimming, and adding water as needed. Add potatoes and cook for 30 minutes more. Add sherry and soy sauce, cook for 20 minutes more. Season to taste with salt and pepper and serve with crusty bread and white jug wine. You'll notice we didn't mention the bones—take 'em out if you're having company.

Note: You can finish off the wine and bread with Brie for a wonderful dessert.

Natha Lee's Chicken and Dumplings

Legendary stuff! Folks drop blatant hints for dinner invitations. Children and small animals get trampled in the stampede when the dinner bell rings.

3–4 pounds chicken, cut and rinsed
3–4 carrots, cut crosswise into 1/2-inch rounds

1 medium onion, diced
1 bay leaf
Pinch of thyme
Salt and pepper to taste

Combine all ingredients in a large pot. Cover with water, bring to boil, and reduce heat to simmer. Cook, uncovered, for 2-1/2 hours or until chicken is tender. Skim foam and excess fat as necessary. Remove bones from chicken and return meat to pot with broth.

(left) Lightly drop small spoonfuls on simmering liquid.

(below) Dinnertime!

FOR THE DUMPLINGS:
1-1/2 cups flour
2 tsp. baking powder
1/2 tsp. salt
3 Tbs. shortening
3/4 cup milk

Combine flour, baking powder, and salt in bowl. Cut in shortening until mixture looks like meal. Make a well in flour mixture, add milk. Mix until all flour is moistened, but do not overmix. Drop dough by spoonfuls *onto meat* in the simmering broth. Cook uncovered for 10 minutes. Cover and cook for another 10 minutes. Serves 6 adults or 2 teenage boys.

Hints: Dumplings will fall apart if cooked in broth that is boiling too hard, so make sure your broth is at a simmer. This dumpling recipe can be doubled, but not tripled as there won't be enough room in the pot for the dough to expand.

Hunter's Stew

Okay, this is the one you've all been waiting for! **Freestyle— no rules! Cook as catch can!** Ducks, dove, deer, feral hog, wild sheep, squirrel, turkey, rabbit, armadillo, exotics, the odd lost goose—you name it. I'd just as soon you saved the quail for another occasion, but if you only have 2 or 3, what the heck?

Start by soaking the heavier meats (venison, sheep, hog) in about 2 cups *cheap* red wine (Gallo Hearty Burgundy is a nice choice) plus 1 Tbs. soy sauce for 3-4 pounds of meat. Soak the meat for about 2 hours. (No red wine you say? Use a can of Lone Star Beer and a 6-oz. bottle of soy sauce.) Drain and flour meat and brown in the morning's bacon grease, sausage grease, or cooking oil (first two choices are best). Add water to cover and add 2 peeled, chopped onions, 1/2 Tbs. garlic powder, 1/2 Tbs. black pepper, 1 tsp. celery salt, and 1 Tbs. Worcestershire sauce, and either 1/2 cup beer or red wine—whichever you used for a marinade. Simmer for 1 hour.

Add quartered squirrel, rabbit, ducks, dove breasts, and quail breasts—whatever you have that's been cleaned, washed, and patted dry. Add water and either beer or wine (about 1/2 cup), cover and simmer for another hour, watching to keep plenty of water in the pot. Meanwhile, make a dark roux using 1 cup flour and one cup of oil, cooking over low heat. When dark enough, add to stew. Simmer covered for 30 to 45 minutes after adding roux. Add several dashes of Tabasco sauce to taste.

Meanwhile, make a *big* pot of real mashed potatoes (about 2 big spuds per person plus two for the pot). Put a large mound of mashed potatoes on each plate. Make a well in the center of the potatoes and ladle a large serving of stew and gravy into the well. Salt to your taste.

Note: Those of you with a quick eye will observe that, with the exception of soy sauce, the spices and condiments are integral to the mandatory Bloody Mary. That ain't by accident, friends!

Venison Stew

2 lbs. venison, cubed
1 cup red wine, non-vintage of course

2 onions, chopped
1 bay leaf
2 garlic cloves, crushed
2 tsp. black pepper
2 onions, sliced thin
6 carrots, sliced thin
1/2 cup parsley, chopped
1 tsp. thyme
1 tsp. oregano
2 cups finely grated potato

In a small saucepan combine wine, onion, bay leaf, garlic cloves, and pepper. Bring to a boil, remove from heat, and allow to cool. Pour marinade over venison in a non-reactive bowl. Allow to marinate for 4 hours. In a Dutch oven, combine drained meat, 1/2 cup of marinade, beef broth, onions, carrots, parsley, thyme, oregano, and grated potato. Add water to cover, cover with lid, and simmer until meat is very tender—about 2 hours. Serve over buttered noodles.

CHILI

About Chili Peppers and Powders

We are blessed (overrun?) with a huge selection of peppers of various descriptions and heat factors. Oftentimes I'll make reference to a light chili powder or dark chili powder. This reference is not purely based on color. Most dark chili powders have a large portion of their makeup derived from the *ancho* chili pepper, which is the dried form of the *poblano* pepper. It has a very dark, rich chili taste and aroma. Commercial varieties in this area include McCormick, Adams, and several available from Pendery's Spice Company of Ft. Worth.

The light powders are primarily derived from the dried New Mexico red pepper (Anaheim) of which there are about a zillion different varieties and growers throughout the Southwest. Commercial powders of this type include Gebhardt, Bolner's Fiesta brand, and a selection available from Pendery's. While the light powders don't have the depth of flavor of the *ancho,* they add a classy touch and finish to the dishes where they are used, and they won't overwhelm you the way the dark powders can if you tip the can too much. Jalapeños and serranos are available either fresh or canned in *escabeche* (seasoned oil). They have all of the heat that the *normal* person needs, and should be approached with care by the uninitiated. Once you have used them a few times, you'll find your own comfort range.

Cayennes are usually found dried and ground, labeled Cayenne Pepper, Red Pepper, or something like that. Cayenne is one of the foundation spices of Cajun cooking, and an excellent source of latent heat for many dishes, from eggs to chili. Green cayennes are less common, but when located are a valuable addition to many dishes, as they lack the absolute heat of the dried version, and carry a distinctive flavor to a dish.

Other peppers that are mentioned are *cascabels* (Mexican and South Texas origin) which are available either whole dried or in powder form and are *very* hot; *chipotles* (jalapeños that have been dried over smoke) are pungent, but not real hot; and the *habanero,* which is the ultimate in hot, beyond planetary bounds. Most of these can be found with a little searching. You'll discover that the more you use them, the easier they are to use. But remember the old line about how porcupines make love . . . *carefully!*

Peppers, *clockwise from top center:* Ancho (dried Poblano), Anaheim, New Mexico Red (dried Anaheim), Cascabel, Jalapeño, Poblano, and, *center,* Serrano.

 Chili

The official state dish of Texas! Chili preparation—what's right and wrong—has inspired arguments, fights, and an International Championship at Terlingua (a ghost town in deep West Texas, just west of Big Bend National Park). The Chili Appreciation

Society International sanctions over 400 chili cook-offs throughout the United States, Canada, Mexico, and the Caribbean. While
the recipe that follows may not win any championships, it's a
variation of a recipe that *has* won—often!

6 lbs. very lean chuck, ground
2 large onions, minced
6 cloves garlic, crushed through a press
6 jalapeño peppers (fresh), stemmed and pierced
Two 8-oz. cans tomato sauce
1 qt. beef broth
6 Tbs. dark chili powder *(ancho)*
4 Tbs. ground *comino*
1/8–1/4 tsp. *habanero* sauce, optional
6 Tbs. light chili powder (New Mexico Red)
1-1/2 tsp. salt
2 Tbs, paprika
1 tsp. white pepper
1 tsp. cayenne pepper
1-1/2 tsp. oregano
1 Tbs. MSG (optional)
1 Tbs. garlic powder

Brown meat in a skillet, drain and put in large (7 qt.) pot. Add
onions, garlic, jalapeños, beef broth, 1 can tomato sauce, dark
chili powder, 2 Tbs. comino, and habanero sauce. Bring to low
boil, cover, and cook for 45 minutes, adding a little water as necessary. Add light chili powder, 1 can tomato sauce, 2 Tbs. *comino,*
and everything else. Simmer covered for 45 minutes. Adjust salt
to taste and serve with cold beer.

Notes: "Very lean" means either you or your butcher have
removed all of the fat and connective tissue. "Ground" means

one trip through the largest grinding plate available and nothing smaller than 1/2 inch. If no plate of sufficient size is available, hand cut the meat into 3/8 to 1/2-inch cubes. That's how trail drive cooks made it for years. If you use cubed meat, extend the first cooking time to 1–1/2 hours to allow the meat to become tender.

More Notes: Habanero sauce is available in many stores, and all over Mexico. Beware! The stuff is so hot it should be a controlled substance! Work up to your own comfort level gradually or omit altogether.

ON THE SUBJECT OF BEANS:

Ah, the humble bean. Cheap, tasty, nutritious; generally an all-around "good guy" in the diet. *But,* there's one place it doesn't belong—cooked in your chili. And why is that, pray tell? Because chili is defined as "meat stewed with peppers and spices." Put another way, when competition chili is being judged one of the criteria from the Chili Appreciation Society International, Inc., rulebook states, *"No fillers in chili*—No beans, macaroni, rice, hominy, or other similar items will be acceptable."

Now, I've got nothing against a bowl of beans *on the side.* Matter of fact, I think it's a darn good idea. So's a couple of jalapeños, a couple of cold beers, and a double fistful of crackers!

So when you crank up the chili pot, just remember what Martindale (Texas) songwriter Kent Finlay had to say on the subject: "If you know beans about chili/You know that chili has no beans."

Competition Style Chili

This particular recipe did extremely well for several years at the cook-offs. Judges' tastes have changed, and they're looking for something different these days, but this is still a good pot of chili. Maybe what we need is a better breed of judge!

3 lbs. chuck tender, trimmed of all waste and cut into 3/8-inch cubes

1 Tbs. fine minced kidney fat

1 large onion, minced fine

6 cloves garlic, peeled and crushed through a press

3 fresh jalapeños, stemmed and pierced

1 14-oz. can beef broth

2 Tbs. finely minced cilantro leaves

2 *chipotle* peppers

1 Lone Star Beer (no substitutes)

2 Tbs. *ancho* chili powder (dark red)

1 Tbs. cumin

6 Tbs. fine ground New Mexico Red chili peppers (light red)

One 8-oz. can tomato sauce

1 Tbs. ground cumin

1/4 tsp. oregano

2 tsp. MSG

1-1/2 tsp. salt

1/2 tsp. ground cayenne pepper

1 tsp. garlic powder

1/2 tsp. white pepper

4 tsp. paprika

1/8 tsp. *cascabel* pepper powder

Put kidney fat in a 4-5 quart Dutch oven that has been pre-heated. When the fat starts to sizzle and gives up its oil, add onion and garlic and sauté for about 2 minutes. Add meat and sauté until meat is browned. Add cilantro, beer, broth, jalapeños, *ancho* powder, cumin, and *chipotles*. Bring to a fast simmer, covered, for 1-1/2 to 1-3/4 hours, adding a little water as needed. Turn off and allow to steep for 1 hour. Discard the *chipotles* and jalapeños at the end of the steeping period. Turn on heat to a low simmer and add everything but the *cascabel* pepper. Simmer covered for 20 minutes, watching the liquid closely. Turn off for 45 minutes. Fifteen minutes before turn-in time, re-ignite the fire and bring to a slow simmer, adding the *cascabel* pepper and any salt you think it needs. Season your cup and turn in, hoping for the best.

Carne Guisada

2 lbs. lean, boneless pork, cut into 3/4-inch cubes
2 lbs. lean, boneless beef, cut into 3/4-inch cubes
Oil for browning
2 onions, peeled and chopped
5 cloves garlic, minced
1 cup flour (or more, as needed)
1 Tbs. cumin
1 jalapeño, minced
Salt and pepper to taste

Combine flour and cumin in a large paper bag. Add meat and shake bag to coat the meat with flour. Heat oil in Dutch oven until very hot, and brown the floured meat. Add onions, garlic, and jalapeño with water to cover. Cover and slowly simmer for 2 hours. Thicken with remaining cumin seasoned flour if desired. Serve with flour tortillas and Spanish rice.

Green Chili Stew

1-1/2 lbs. very lean pork, coarsely ground or cubed
1-1/2 lbs. lean beef, coarsely ground or cubed
1 large onion, coarsely chopped
2 cloves garlic, minced
1 cup green chiles (Anaheims), stemmed and coarsely chopped
2 tsp cumin
1 cup tomatoes, peeled and chopped
2 Tbs. oil
1 fresh jalapeño, stemmed and diced

Brown pork, beef, onion, and garlic in 2 Tbs. oil using a large Dutch oven. Add green chiles, jalapeño, cumin, and tomatoes. Stir to blend. Add water to cover, bring to a boil, and cook at a slow boil, covered, for 45 minutes to 1 hour for ground meats and 1–1/2 to 2 hours for cubed meats. Serve in bowls with warm flour tortillas on the side. A side serving of *posole* is great with this—see below.

Carne Adovado

A staple of Southwestern cooking, this requires overnight marinating but little actual work. While we used pork butt roast (it was on sale!), pork steaks, thick pork chops, or any other cut of fresh pork will work just as well.

4 cups dried New Mexico red peppers, seeded, stemmed,
    torn into bits
Water
1 tsp. garlic powder
1-1/2 tsp. cumin
3-1/4 lbs. boneless pork butt roast, cut into 1-1/2 inch
    cubes
1 large onion, finely chopped

In a stainless-steel pan, combine peppers and water to cover,
bring to a boil, cover, and remove from heat. Allow to steep for
1 hour. Strain peppers, reserving liquid. Puree peppers in a food
processor, adding enough to the cooking liquid to reach a tomato
sauce consistency. Stir in garlic powder and cumin. Place meat
in a non-reactive bowl and add pureed peppers. Toss meat to
thoroughly coat. Cover and refrigerate over night.

    Preheat oven to 275°. Add onion to meat mixture and stir
thoroughly. Pour into a non-reactive baking dish, and bake
covered, for 2-1/2 hours. Serves 6.

Posole

    Posole—aka dried hominy—is a great side dish for spicy
dishes like green chili stew and carne adovada, and a staple of
Southwestern cuisine. It's hard to find in supermarkets, but the
folks listed in the Appendix can help you out with a mail order.
Since it's dried, it stores well in your pantry, so you can order
a bunch!

2 cups dried posole (about 12 oz. net wt.)
8 cups water
1 smoked pork hock

1 large onion, chopped
3 large cloves garlic, crushed through a press
3 Tbs. cumin
1 tsp. salt

Combine posole, water, pork hock, onion, garlic, and half the cumin. Bring to a boil, reduce heat, and simmer covered for two hours. Add remaining cumin and the salt, and simmer for 2 to 3 hours longer. Serves 8.

Caution: Watch the water level, adding a little additional, as needed.

— SIDE DISHES AND VEGGIES —

Ham 'n' Butter Beans

My dad always thought you ought to have equal parts ham and beans. While this doesn't quite get there, it's close!

2 lbs. dry butter beans, picked over and washed
1 lb. smoked ham shank, including bone
1 large onion, peeled and chopped
Black pepper to taste

In a 4–5 quart pot, bring 2 quarts of water to a boil. Add ham shank and simmer slowly for 1 hour. Add beans, onions, and cover with water. Cover pot and simmer slowly for 2 to 2-1/2 hours, adding water as needed, or until beans are thoroughly soft. Serves 6–8 as main course. Serve with turnip greens, cornbread, green onions, and fruit cobbler.

Green Beans and New Potatoes

2 lbs. fresh green beans (Kentucky Wonders, or whatever looks good), washed, stringed, and snapped
1-1/2 lbs. small red potatoes, washed (use potatoes about the size of an egg)
1/2 lb. salt pork, sliced thin (or bacon ends, or ham hocks)
1 large onion, peeled and sliced
1 clove garlic, peeled and crushed
Salt and pepper to taste

Combine salt pork and 2 qts. of water in pot with onion and garlic. Bring to a boil, reduce heat, and simmer covered for 20 minutes. Add beans, simmer for 20 minutes. Add potatoes (whole if small, halved if tennis-ball size) and simmer for an additional 25 minutes. Add salt and pepper to taste—don't salt before now; remember, the salt pork is in there. Serves 6.

Prize-Winnin' Pintos

Lots of folks have used this recipe over the years in a variety of cook-offs with a lot of success. While it may be simplistic, it's also very reliable.

2 lbs. dry pintos
1/2 lb. salt pork, cubed 1 by 1 by 1/4 inch
1 Tbs. chili powder
2 medium onions, chopped
2 cloves garlic, minced

1/2 tsp. cayenne
1 tsp. black pepper
2 canned jalapeños (optional)

Soak the beans overnight. Drain. Fill with water to cover and add everything else to pot. Cook *very* slow for 4–6 hours. When beans are done, test for salt and adjust to your preference. Don't salt in advance, because the salt pork will do that for you!

Serve with cornbread, green onions, and beer—or as a side dish with nearly anything else in this book.

Blackeyed Peas and Sausage

Good any time of the year, this is a great dish for New Year's Day. Even minds that have been simpled by the frivolity of the season can cope with the preparation. Serve with cabbage steamed in chicken broth and you have taken care of all your nutritional needs, as well as answered the requirements of the pagan rites associated with the day.

1 lb. dried blackeyed peas
1 large onion, chopped
1 lb. smokey link sausage (Carltons, Opa's, Smoke A Roma, etc.)
1 fresh jalapeño, stemmed and pierced

Rinse peas, place in a pot with water to cover, bring to a boil, cover and turn off the heat. Allow to "set" for an hour as peas swell. Add onion, garlic, jalapeño, and sausage sliced into 1-inch lengths. Simmer, covered, for 1–1/2 hours, or until peas are tender but not mushy. Serve with cornbread, and green onions.

Okra Gumbo

One of the joys of summer—when everything is as fresh as possible. Choose okra pods 3-inches long or shorter (the big ones are tougher than a banker's heart).

  2-1/2 cups fresh okra, sliced crosswise 1/2-inch thick
  1-1/2 cups fresh tomatoes, peeled and chopped
  1 large onion, chopped
  2 slices bacon

Brown bacon in a Dutch oven. Remove and drain. Pour off drippings, leaving 2 Tbs. in the Dutch oven. Lightly sauté onions in the drippings, add okra and water to cover. Simmer covered for 10 minutes. Add tomatoes and simmer covered for 30 minutes. Serves 6.

Spanish Rice

  2 cups rice
  1/2 cup chopped onion
  1/2 cup chopped celery
  5 cloves garlic, crushed
  3 serrano peppers, stemmed and chopped
  2 Tbs. oil
  Oil for browning rice
  One 13-3/4 oz. can chicken broth
  One 10-oz. can Rotel tomatoes, liquified in a blender
  One 8-oz. can tomato sauce

1/2 cup water

1 tsp. cumin (or more, to suit yourself)

Slowly sauté onion, celery, garlic, and serranos in 2 Tbs. oil until softened. Set aside. In a large skillet, heat 3 Tbs. oil until nearly smoking. Add 1 cup rice and stir constantly until browned. Add 1/2 onion mixture to rice, heat through, and then throw in a 4-quart pot with lid. (Remove the lid first.) Repeat with remaining rice and onion mixture. Add broth, tomatoes, tomato sauce, cumin, and water to pot. Bring to a boil, reduce heat to low, and cook covered tightly till all moisture is absorbed. Serves 8–10.

Texas Vegetable Medley

This is a serious side dish for barbecue.

1 pkg. frozen corn cobettes (12 count) or 6 fresh ears, cleaned and broken into halves

1 dozen red new potatoes, washed (leave unpeeled and whole)

8 golf-ball sized white boiler onions, peeled

1 pkg. Shrimp and Crab Boil

2 sticks butter or margarine (melted)

In a 10–12 quart pot, bring 8 quarts of water to a rolling boil. Toss in the bag of Shrimp and Crab Boil (unopened) and boil for 10 minutes. Add corn and return to boil for 7 minutes. Add whole potatoes and onions and return to boil for 25 minutes or until potatoes are done, whichever comes first. Drain off all liquid, place veggies in a serving dish, and slather with butter. Serves 8.

Turnip Greens with Turnips

Texas produces turnips in large quantities during the cooler months. When you bring your bagful home, cut the turnips off, remove and discard the tough lower stems, then wash the leaves in cool water, drain the sink, and re-wash. Amazing how much sand is in those leaves, ain't it?

    2 bunches turnips with greens
    3/4 lb. salt pork, cut into large dice
    2 onions, peeled and sliced

After you've rinsed the turnip leaves, peel and cube the turnips. Sauté the salt pork with the onions for about 5–6 minutes in a large Dutch oven. Add turnips and greens and cover with water. Simmer over low heat, covered, for about 1–1/2 to 2–1/2 hours. Serves 4–6. Serve with cornbread to soak up the "pot likker."

Sesame Spinach

    2 pkgs. frozen spinach
    2/3 stick margarine
    Juice of half a lemon
    2-1/2 Tbs. sesame seeds

Toast sesame seeds for 8 minutes in a 350° oven. Prepare spinach according to package instructions. Drain spinach, add butter, and toss. Squeeze on lemon juice and toss. Add *hot* sesame seeds, toss lightly, and serve immediately. Serves 4. Natha and Dorothy Wilson like this one, big time!

ENTREES

Braised Leg of Pig

    1 5-lb. pork shoulder roast
    6 sprigs rosemary
    1 onion, sliced
    2 apples, cored and cut into eighths
    1/2 Tbs. garlic powder
    4 fresh cayenne peppers (green)
    1 13-oz. can chicken broth

Place roast in a large Dutch oven. Surround and cover with rosemary, onion slices, apple pieces, and cayenne peppers. Sprinkle with garlic powder. Pour chicken broth over all and simmer covered for 2-1/2–3 hrs. Serves 4–6.

Chicken Tacos

    There are two versions of chicken tacos—*pollo al carbon* (grilled) and this one, similar in nature to *carne guisada*. If you prefer the grilled method, then warm up some flour tortillas, put out a bowl of *pico de gallo,* and use the recipe found under "Grilling—Chicken Breasts."

    3-4 lbs. chicken or selected chicken parts
    2 onions, peeled and chopped
    3 cloves garlic, peeled and crushed
    1 carrot, diced

1 fresh jalapeño, stemmed and minced
1 fresh serrano, stemmed and minced
3/4 tsp. oregano
1 Tbs. cumin
1 bay leaf
Two 13-3/4 oz. cans chicken broth

Combine everything in a large pot and add enough water to cover. Bring to a boil. Reduce heat, cover and simmer for 1 to 1-1/2 hours. Allow to cool, strain, and remove bones. Serve in the center of the table with warmed flour tortillas, side dishes of *pico de gallo*, guacamole, and Spanish rice.

Pot Roast

One of the great comfort foods of our time. Anybody that doesn't like pot roast probably has other serious character flaws as well.

3-5 lb. chuck roast
2-3 medium onions, peeled and quartered
1 lb. carrots, scraped and quartered
3 lbs. potatoes, scrubbed and quartered lengthwise
    (leave the peelings on)
4 stalks celery, chunked
1/2 small head cabbage, quartered
1 bay leaf
1/2 tsp. thyme
1 tsp. garlic powder

Sear roast on both sides in a large skillet. Place in Dutch oven, add half the onions, bay leaf, thyme, and garlic powder, cover with water, and simmer on top of stove for about 2 hours. Add celery, carrots, cabbage, and rest of onions. Replace lid and continue cooking for 45 minutes. Add potatoes and cook covered until potatoes are tender (about 25 minutes). Remove meat and vegetables from Dutch oven. Thicken gravy with cornstarch (about 2 Tbs. dissolved in 4 oz. cold water) and pass on the side.

Hint: A truly caring person would have homemade biscuits or a yeast bread to go with this!

Potted Doves

The name refers to the cooking method, not the condition of the birds when cooked! Actually, doves are among the most expensive fowl around, when you consider the number of shotgun shells it takes to gather a pound of dove meat.

12 dove breasts, skinned, washed, and patted dry
6 slices bacon, quartered
1-1/2 to 2 cups flour
2 Tbs. black pepper
1 onion, peeled and cut into eighths
3 Tbs. dry sherry

In a large Dutch oven, sauté the bacon over medium heat until crisp. Remove with a slotted spoon. Combine flour and black pepper in a paper bag. Drop dove breasts into bag, close top, and shake to coat breasts with flour. Brown floured breasts in hot bacon drippings. Remove breasts when browned and, using remaining seasoned flour, make about 2 quarts of brown water gravy. When gravy is made, return breasts to pot, add onion and sherry, cover, and simmer over low heat for 1 hour (longer if birds aren't tender). Add crisp bacon to gravy for extra flavor. Serves 4. Serve over rice.

Brown Water Gravy

Brown about 1/4 cup seasoned flour in 3 or 4 tablespoons of drippings. Cook until golden brown. Slowly add 6–8 cups boiling water, stirring constantly, until gravy is thickened. Makes approximately 2 quarts of gravy. Additional water can be added if gravy seems to be getting too thick.

Smothered Game

Thin slices of venison, feral hog, or Barbados sheep hams should be floured and browned as in the potted dove recipe above. When you make the gravy, add 1 cup of the leftover morning coffee and boiling water. The coffee will tenderize the meat and add richness. Always use about 1 lb. onions to 2–3 lbs. of meat and simmer slowly.

Homemade biscuits are really a treat with this. Good biscuits will get you permanent cooking duty, but a tough negotiator will get rid of all the other chores, including KP.

Pork Roast with Sauerkraut

4 lbs. pork roast, butt or loin
2 medium onions, peeled and quartered
2 apples, stemmed and quartered
Black pepper
Garlic powder
One 13-3/4 oz. can chicken broth
2 qts. sauerkraut (use the kind in jars from the refrigerated
      section of your store; canned just doesn't get the job
      done)

Sprinkle black pepper and garlic powder over roast and place fat side up in a Dutch oven with lid. Add apple and onion to pan and 1 can chicken broth. Cover and cook in the oven at 300 degrees for 1-1/2 hours. Pour sauerkraut over the roast, cover, and continue cooking for 1 hour longer. Serves 4-6.

Note: This works real well in a slowcooker, too! Serve with horseradish sauce on the side.

Horseradish Sauce

1 cup sour cream
4 Tbs. prepared horseradish
1 Tbs. mayonnaise

Combine all ingredients at least one hour before serving. Cover tightly and store in the refrigerator.

Taos Pork Chops

4 loin pork chops, 3/4-inch thick
Two 4-oz. cans whole green chilies
1/2 large onion, sliced (a Texas 1015 is perfect)
8 oz. shredded Monterey Jack cheese
3/4 tsp. cumin
1/2 tsp. garlic powder
3/4 of a 13-3/4 oz. can chicken broth (approximately)

Sear each pork chop in a skillet for 1 minute on each side, then place in a covered Dutch oven large enough to hold all the chops in a single layer. Sprinkle the onions evenly over the chops. Split open the chilies and use them to cover the tops of the chops.

In a small bowl, mix the juice from the two cans of chilies with the garlic and cumin. Pour chili juice mixture into Dutch oven, adding enough chicken broth to bring the liquid 3/4 of the way up on the chops. Cover, bring to a boil on top of the stove, reduce heat, and simmer for 15 minutes. Remove lid, sprinkle cheese over top of chops, and slide the Dutch oven into a preheated broiler oven for about five minutes or until cheese melts and is bubbly. Serves 4 normal people or two like me.

Note: This recipe also works well with chicken breasts!

Poached Chicken Breasts

4 chicken breast halves with ribs
1 large sweet onion, peeled, halved, and sliced
1/2 lb. mushrooms, stemmed and sliced

4 Tbs. butter
One 13-3/4 oz. can chicken broth
1 Tbs. fresh rosemary or 2 tsp. dried

Sauté onions and mushrooms in 2 Tbs. butter over medium heat for 5 to 6 minutes until softened. Remove from pan and reserve. Add 2 Tbs. butter and brown the chicken breasts on both sides. Add the chicken broth, the mushrooms, onions, and rosemary to the pan. Cover, bring to a boil, reduce heat, and simmer for 20 minutes. Serves 4.

Your Basic Meatloaf

2 lbs. ground beef
1 can tomato sauce
1 egg, beaten
1 onion, minced
1 bell pepper, minced
1 Tbs. Worcestershire sauce
1 tsp. garlic powder
Dash Tabasco sauce
2 slices bread, toasted and crumbed

In a large bowl mix all ingredients except tomato sauce. Your hands work better than a spoon for this. Spread evenly in a Dutch oven (not cast iron). Bake at 350° for 45 minutes. Spread tomato sauce on top of meatloaf and return to oven for an additional 15 minutes. Serve with mashed potatoes and steamed spinach.

Meatloaf, Basic Southwestern Variety

2 lbs. ground beef
1 onion, peeled and chopped
1 can Rotel tomatoes and chilies
2 cloves garlic, peeled and crushed
1 egg, beaten
2 slices bread, toasted and crumbed
2 fresh serranos, minced
1 fresh jalapeño, minced
1/2 tsp. cumin
1 can tomato sauce
1 small can whole green chilies

Combine first nine ingredients in a large bowl, mixing thoroughly. Spread evenly in Dutch oven (not cast iron). Top with whole green chilies. Spread tomato sauce on top. Bake at 350° for 45 minutes to one hour. Serves 4–6 with leftovers for sandwiches.

Texas Style Swiss Steak

2 to 2-1/2 lbs. round steak, 3/4-inch thick
One 14-1/2 oz. can whole peeled tomatoes
2 medium onions, peeled and sliced
2 to 4 fresh serrano peppers, stemmed and minced (for a
        milder taste substitute one small can green chilies)
3/4 tsp. cumin
3 cloves garlic, peeled and minced
1/2 tsp. crumbled dried oregano

1 can beef broth
Salt and pepper to taste

Remove fat and connective tissue from meat and cut into serving-size pieces. Sear meat pieces on each side in a skillet and add meat to a 4-5 quart Dutch oven. Combine tomatoes and their juice, onions, peppers, cumin, garlic, oregano, and beef broth in a bowl. Mix to blend and pour over meat. Add necessary water to cover meat. Bring to a boil, cover, reduce heat, and simmer slowly for 1-1/2 to 2 hours or until very tender. Serves 4. Serve with rice or mashed potatoes.

Note: If you like the flavor, a tablespoon of minced cilantro can be mixed in during the last half hour of cooking.

Shrimp Boil

Shrimp boil is best done outside. A Coleman stove (or fish fryer) is the ideal cooking unit. It's also best done with shrimp as fresh as possible. May we recommend an alfresco affair on the beach?

8 lbs. shrimp, headed
1 bag Shrimp and Crab Boil
1 large green salad, premixed and chilled, with dressing
    added at last minute
1 qt. red sauce (recipe below)
1 beer cooler, filled with ice and beer

Bring a large (16-20 quart) pot of water to a boil. Add Shrimp Boil, return to boil for ten minutes. Add shrimp, bring to boil for seven minutes. Kill fire and allow shrimp to sit in hot water for 10 minutes. Add dressing to salad. Drain shrimp and dump into a large bowl. This is a "u peel 'um" affair. Serve beer throughout the whole process. If you prefer, you can ice the shrimp for an hour before serving. Serve with red sauce and salad. 6–8 servings.

Red Sauce for Shrimp and Oysters

Texas is blessed with a long and beautiful Gulf Coast. Two gems of the sea are its shrimp and oyster populations. They are best enjoyed simply—oysters on the half shell and boiled shrimp are staple fare, at least for me. Here's a red sauce that goes with either shrimp or oysters. It's a little piquant for some folks, so work up to your own level:

    1 cup catsup
    One 8-oz. bottle chili sauce
    3–4 Tbs. prepared horseradish
    Juice of 1 lemon
    1/2 tsp. garlic powder
    Tabasco sauce to taste

Combine everything together, taste, and adjust to suit yourself. If it's too hot, smooth it out with more catsup. Refrigerate for an hour or more to mellow flavors.

Chapter Three
Stuff You Cook In A Skillet

First, we gotta cure a *large* misconception. Everything that's cooked in a skillet isn't fried, and everything that's fried isn't cooked in a skillet. A skillet is one of the most versatile tools in the kitchen and you should have a variety of sizes and materials—all good quality—at your disposal. As we get further into this section, we'll talk more about specifics, but there is one rule of thumb that you can apply: Given equal size, the lighter the skillet, the less desirable it is—to the point of worthlessness. We've got one around our house that is so poor that it'll scorch water. Makes a good dog food bowl, though.

Cast-iron skillets require a little tender loving care and, of course, a proper seasoning. They hold and spread the heat more evenly, and are usually deep enough for any frying job. Their weight is a deterrent to some cooks, but for general skillet jobs they're the first choice. They also put a crust on cornbread that can't be beat (see cornbread recipe elsewhere).

Next in line would be the heavy aluminum skillets with a non-stick surface. They clean up in a hurry and do an excellent job. As a rule, if you kind of choke up when you glance at the price tag, you're probably in the right area. I've never seen a quality skillet at a discount store, and God knows I've looked! Pure stainless steel is not a good choice, since it is a poor conductor of heat; however, stainless steel with aluminum clad bottoms are excellent utensils (see chapter on second mortgages).

There are specialty skillets of countless descriptions for various special applications—omelette pans of various descriptions, oval, special side angles, folding sides, etc. Others include low-sided griddle skillets, square (I never have figured that one out—it seems that you wouldn't want any corners to catch and hold debris, but who am I to gripe?), and the wok, which is a highly specialized skillet that has evolved over the centuries in the Far East—and that's a very useful addition to your toolbox. Your wok can be used for a whole lot more than just stir frying. Give serious thought to one of these. There are electric and stove-fired varieties; mine is the latter, and having used both, I prefer the stove-fired variety. Even as this is written, I'm plotting a way to create a "gorilla-sized" wok for use over my large outdoor cooker.

Part of the author's arsenal. *From left, front:* wok, 12" cast iron, 8" cast iron, 12" electric stainless steel; *back:* 14" cast-iron griddle, 12" nonstick aluminum, 10" nonstick aluminum.

Whatever you happen to have, that's what you'll start with and all of these other things will find their way into your kitchen, until you develop a storage problem. Regardless, just as with the barbecue pits, it's not what kind you have, but how well you learn to use them! With that in mind, choose your weapon, and let's cook something.

───── *FRYING—A PRIMER* ─────

Fried foods have taken a lot of knocks over the years from various health folks because of greasiness, cholesterol, etc. The fact is that if frying is done correctly, it's not nearly as objectionable as these folks would have you believe. By the way, did you ever notice that most of those folks who are so concerned about your health are trying to sell you something?

Here's some handy tips for doin' it right:

1. Always use fresh, high-quality oil for frying—Wesson or Crisco are the norm, but nearly any good oil will work. Lard can be used, but it needs care or you will add the bad "C word" to your cooking.

2. Use enough oil to do the job. Many people try to get away with 3–5 tablespoons of oil in a big skillet to cut down on the grease. The fact is that you need 1/4 to 1/2 inch of oil to seal the batter. If the batter doesn't seal, the food absorbs more oil. It's not how much oil you *use*, it's how much oil the food *absorbs* that matters.

3. The primary mistake that most people make when they unlimber the skillet is that they *never get the oil hot enough!* To fry properly, the oil needs to be at least 360°, and 375°

is preferable, *before* you start to put food into it. (Around MED-HIGH on an electric range.) When frying more than one batch, always allow the oil to return to the desired temperature between batches.

4. Don't crowd items being fried. Crowding causes steam, which in turn melts off the batter, making greasy food.

5. When possible, refrigerate breaded or battered foods for 20–30 minutes prior to cooking to "set" the outer coating.

6. Always drain immediately upon removing food from the skillet. Paper towels tend to make foods soggy; instead, use a wire rack over a catch pan for much crisper, less greasy foods.

7. Choose your weapon wisely! The first choice here is a large, deep, well-seasoned cast-iron skillet.

I'm through preachin' now, so you can go ahead and start dinner. We'll begin with a genuine classic!

Chicken-Fried Steak and Gravy

In most of Texas, and many parts of the Southwest, chicken-fried steak is considered a basic food group all by itself, and the gravy is an integral part—if the gravy is lousy, so's the meal. A well-prepared chicken-fried steak is hard to find—as are most good things in life. It was the first thing I went looking for after too long in the Big Apple. Well-l-l, maybe the second. I do seem to recall a double order of enchiladas and a couple of good cold longnecks in there.

Anyhow, a large tip of the black felt to Natha for the gravy recipe. She is, in my opinion, one of the great gravymakers of our time.

> 2 lbs. boneless round steak, about 1/2 inch thick (sirloin tip also works nicely), trimmed of all fat, and cut into serving-size pieces
> 1 cup flour (or more, as needed)
> 1 Tbs. black pepper
> 1 tsp. thyme
> 1 tsp. oregano
> 1/2 tsp. garlic powder
> 1 egg, lightly beaten
> 1 cup milk
> Oil for frying

Pound meat with a meat mallet or heavy knife (or have your butcher run it through his meat tenderizer, if he's got one). Sprinkle meat with a little flour and pound lightly again. Do both sides. Thoroughly mix flour, pepper, thyme, oregano, and garlic powder in a shallow bowl. Combine milk and egg in another shallow bowl. Dip floured meat into milk mixture and dredge it in the seasoned flour, making sure that both sides are well coated. Chill while the oil is heating. Heat 1/2 inch oil in a large skillet to 375°. Place meat in hot oil, but do not crowd.

Cook until golden brown on one side, turn and cook until brown on the other side. Remove to a rack, and repeat with the rest of the meat, allowing the oil to return to the proper temperature each time before you add another batch of meat. When the meat is cooked and the gravy made, pour a generous dollop of gravy over each serving and pass the rest at the table. Potatoes of some sort—mashed, mashed, or mashed, french fries or homefries, a green salad, and plenty of bread to sop up the gravy completes the meal.

FOR THE GRAVY:
Reserve 3-4 Tbs. of the oil used to fry the meat. Don't throw away the little bits of meat and batter that are left in the bottom of the pan. That's what makes the gravy *good*. Sprinkle 4-5 Tbs. flour over the heated oil, salt and pepper to taste, and stir until light brown. Add 3 cups milk slowly, stirring all the time to keep the gravy from getting lumpy. Canned milk which has been mixed with equal parts of water makes the best gravy, 'umm good! Cook over medium heat until the gravy is as thick as you want. Remember that the gravy will get a little thicker as it cools. Remove from heat and serve. Serves 4-6.

Potatoes

Ah, the humble spud—plentiful, cheap, and much maligned in weight-loss circles (wrongly so!), and totally un-chic. Also one of the best loved foods extant! Treat 'em right, and there's nothin' more satisfying.

FRENCH FRIES, STEAK FRIES, ETC.

5 medium potatoes, scrubbed

Slice potatoes lengthwise into roughly equal pieces (so they all get done at the same time). 1/2 by 1/2 inch by potato length is about right. We don't peel 'em, but you can if you wish. There is lots of taste and vitamins in the peel, though. Put cut potatoes in *ice* water for about 15 minutes before frying. Bring about 3/4 inch oil to 375° in a *large skillet*. Drain a panful of potatoes, leaving the rest in the ice water, and *ease* the potatoes into the hot oil. *Watch out for popping oil!* Cook until golden brown, and remove immediately to a rack and season to taste while on the rack. (See note below.) Allow oil to return to the correct temperature and repeat until all potatoes are cooked. Serves 4–6 generously.

Note: Some folks salt their potatoes at this point, while others just use a little cayenne. Whatever suits you is what's right.

HOME FRIES

Not truly fried, this is one of those dishes that many people love, and very few restaurants cook. Hard to beat, this is food for the soul.

> 5 medium potatoes, washed and thinly sliced crossways
> 2 medium onions, peeled, thinly sliced and separated into rings
> Salt and pepper to taste
> Oil for cooking

In a large bowl, mix onions and potatoes together and cover with ice water. In a large skillet with a lid, bring about 1/4 inch oil to 350°. Drain enough potatoes and onions to make about two layers in the bottom of the pan. Ease the potatoes and onions into the pan and cover. When potatoes have browned nicely on the bottom, turn with spatula, recover, and cook until just done. Drain on rack, adding salt and pepper to taste. Repeat as needed to feed your crowd.

Onion Rings

There's several schools of thought about onion rings—some say sliced very thin, some say thick sliced. My choice is medium thick. However, there's no argument about what *kind* of onions to use—*big, sweet ones* win hands down! Texas 1015, Walla Walla, or Vidalias, for example. Another disagreement is seasoned flour versus battered. Since I like 'em both, I put a recipe for each in here.

> 3 large sweet onions, peeled whole and sliced about 3/8
>   inch thick, rings separated, and covered with ice
>   water for about 15 minutes
> Flour mix or batter dip (see recipes below)
> Oil for frying

Heat about 3/4 inch oil to 375° in a very large skillet (use two if you have them). Ease battered or floured onion rings into the skillet and fry to a golden brown. Immediately remove to a draining rack. Repeat with remaining onions. Serves 4–6.

FOR FLOUR DIP:
In a paper bag, combine 1-1/2 cups flour, 1 Tbs. black pepper, and 1/2 tsp. garlic powder. Put a few onion rings (still moist) into the bag, shake to coat, and fry as directed above.

FOR BATTER:
>   1-1/3 cups flour
>   1 egg, beaten
>   1 can beer, room temperature
>   1 tsp. black pepper
>   1/2 tsp. cayenne pepper

Combine all ingredients thoroughly. Drain onion rings and dip into batter, allowing excess to drain off. Fry immediately as directed above.

——— ABOUT DEEP FRYING ———

Just about the time a guy develops the reputation for catching fish in quantity on a regular basis, he discovers that he has a much larger circle of close personal friends who have a keen interest in fried fish. If he tries to satiate this herd with a skillet or two, he'll find himself cooking until midnight and then going to bed hungry! Necessity being the mother of invention, these overworked fisher lads conjured up a home-deep-frying system that will turn out the desired product much more quickly. The theory is the same as the deep fryers found in restaurants, but is much more portable and flexible. The first ones were based on the heating elements of discarded gas water heaters attached to a propane bottle and they worked quite well. As time progressed, the manufacturing segment of our economy caught on, and now there are a variety of portable deep fryers on the market at reasonable prices.

The whole idea of deep frying is to bring a quantity of oil to the proper temperature in a hurry, cook the fish—or whatever—quickly and return the oil to the proper temperature quickly for the next batch. In order to do this you need a heat source considerably stronger than that found on the common household range, hence the special heating unit. Usually, the deep frying container will hold up to two gallons of cooking oil, so you can see that the heat requirements are much higher. The other benefit to having a separate heat source for your deep fryer is that it is most generally used outside, a towering point in your favor at cleanup time.

As a rule, the same guidelines for frying in a skillet apply to deep frying: Wait until the oil is about 375°, don't crowd items being fried, wait until the oil returns to the proper temperature for the next batch, and always drain the finished product on a rack or in a wire basket. But *first* you gotta catch some fish! I'm still working on that part.

Fried Fish

Fish, regardless of how it's cooked, relies on freshness for its flavor. The old cliché of the best fish being cooked streamside has a lot of validity. Modern freezing and handling methods have made fish available to a larger segment of the population, but the freshness rule still applies. Filets are the easiest to work with, but small fish such as perch can be chunked and fried as well. Try to keep each batch uniform in size as you cook. There are two methods that are used—skillet frying and deep frying. Deep frying is the preferred method, but lots of folks don't have the heat source or the pot and basket to do it right, so we'll talk about skillet frying.

2 lbs. fresh fish (filets or chunks), rinsed and patted dry
1 cup flour
1 Tbs. black pepper
1 cup milk
Corn meal
Oil for frying

Combine flour and pepper. Roll fish in the flour mixture. Dip fish into milk and then roll in the cornmeal. Shake off excess and place on a rack for 15 minutes. Heat 1 inch of oil in a large skillet to 375°. Ease fish into the oil, do not crowd. Fry until golden brown on one side and then turn. When the second side is cooked to golden brown, drain on a rack and allow oil to reheat to 375°. Repeat with remaining fish until it is all cooked. Serves 4.

Like tartar sauce? Here's a good basic sauce to build your own from.

1 cup mayonnaise
1/4 cup minced onion
2 Tbs. minced dill pickle
1/4 tsp. cayenne pepper
1/8 tsp. garlic powder

Combine all ingredients and store in refrigerator for 2 or more hours to mellow the flavors.

Butterfly Shrimp

King of the Texas Coast, the shrimp is often abused by many, mostly out of ignorance. Far and away the best way to bread the shrimp is with unseasoned cracker meal. It allows the sweet shrimp taste to shine!

32 large shrimp, 10–15 to the pound
1-1/2 cups cracker meal, more or less
Oil for frying

Head, peel, and devein shrimp, leaving tail section intact (it makes a good handle for eating). Butterfly by cutting 2/3 of the way through the shrimp lengthwise, on the underside. Rinse under cold running water, but do not dry. Press each side into cracker meal, place on a rack, and chill for 30 minutes prior to cooking. Preheat 1 inch oil to 375°. Place shrimp gently into the oil, with tail section sticking up. *Do not crowd.* Fry until golden brown. Remove to a rack and repeat with remaining shrimp.

Oysters

Great food, oysters. I put this in because some folks won't eat 'em the way you're supposed to. After all, each one comes equipped with its own individual serving plate, doesn't it?

3 dozen oysters, shucked, in their liquor
2 cups cracker meal
1 Tbs. black pepper
Oil for frying

Remove a few oysters at a time from their liquor and place immediately into the cracker meal seasoned with the black pepper. Press to make sure that the meal adheres to the oysters. Heat 1 inch of oil to 375°. Add oysters directly from the cracker meal. Fry until golden brown, drain on a rack, and serve immediately with red sauce. (See recipe elsewhere.)

Home-Fried Chicken

Follow the directions under chicken-fried steak for the gravy to go with the mashed potatoes and biscuits that really go well with this.

1 fryer, cut into serving pieces (2-1/2 to 3 lbs.)
1 cup flour
1 Tbs. black pepper
Oil for frying

Combine flour and pepper in a large paper bag and shake. Add chicken parts, a few at a time, and shake to coat. Heat 3/4 inch of oil in a large skillet to 375°. Fry, uncovered, about 45 minutes for the dark meat and about 30 minutes for the white meat. Turn each piece of chicken several times for even browning. Drain on a rack while you're making the gravy.

Fried Green Tomatoes

One of the special pleasures of either having a garden or a handy veggie stand: when tomatoes are abundant, you can get these.

2 large green tomatoes, sliced about 1/2 inch thick
1/2 cup cornmeal
1 egg, beaten
1/2 cup milk
Oil for frying

Combine the egg and milk. Dip the tomatoes into the liquid and then dredge in the cornmeal. Allow the cornmeal to "set." Heat 1/4 inch oil in a heavy skillet to 365°. Place tomatoes in a single layer in the oil; do not crowd. Cook until nicely browned on each side. Remove, drain, and serve immediately. Serves 4.

Note: Use this method on zucchini, yellow squash, or cucumbers for an interesting change.

——— ABOUT OMELETTES ———

Now here's a little something that's too handy to be left to the fern-covered restaurants. Once you learn a couple of tricks and practice a little, you'll be turning out these omelettes like a pro.

First, always have your eggs at room temperature. Beat 3 eggs slightly in a bowl and add 1 Tbs. tap water. Use a 7 or 8 inch non-stick skillet with sloping sides. (They make very expensive omelette pans, but non-stick is much more forgiving!) Heat 2 Tbs. unsalted butter over medium high heat until foam subsides but butter is not browned. Add eggs to pan and cook for 20–30 seconds (until edges set). Gently push edges toward center to allow remaining egg to run to edges and cook while shaking the pan gently. Add fillings while top is still moist. Using either a half fold or triple fold, enclose the filling, and immediately slide onto serving plate. Garnish and serve.

I have included three proven ideas below, but the possibilities are only limited by your imagination. Go for it!

Omelette Oscar

For *each* omelette:

> 5 Tbs. grated Gruyère cheese
> 1/4 cup canned asparagus tips, warmed
> 1/4 cup fresh steamed crabmeat, at room temperature

Sprinkle 3 Tbs. cheese on omelette. Add asparagus and crabmeat. Fold onto plate and sprinkle with the remaining cheese. Serve with fresh strawberries.

Chorizo and Cheese Omelettes

For *two* omelettes:

> 1/2 lb. chorizo (Mexican spicy sausage)
> 2 Tbs. minced onion
> 1/2 cup grated cheese (either Monterey Jack or Longhorn)

Remove casing from chorizo and brown the meat with the onions over medium heat until meat is well browned. Drain thoroughly. To each omelette add 3 Tbs. of the cheese, then half the chorizo mixture. Fold onto serving plates and top with remaining cheese. Serve fresh cantaloupe slices on the side.

Taos Omelettes

For *two* omelettes:

> 2 Tbs. minced onion
> 1 small fresh serrano, stemmed, seeded, and minced
> 1 large tomato, peeled and diced
> 1/2 cup grated Monterey Jack cheese
> 1/2 lb. bulk pork sausage
> One 4-oz. can green chilies, diced

Brown sausage well with onion and serrano. Drain thoroughly. Add chilies to sausage mixture. Top each omelette with 3 Tbs. cheese and half the sausage mixture. Fold onto serving plates and top each with 1 Tbs. cheese and half of the chopped tomato. Serve sliced fresh peaches on the side.

—— OTHER SKILLET STUFF ——

Walk-Through-The-Garden Scrambled Eggs

Here again, this idea came up as the result of what was on hand.

2 Tbs. butter
1 small serrano, stemmed, seeded, and minced
2 green onions, thinly sliced (including the tops)
3 slices American cheese, diced fine
6 eggs, well beaten with 2 Tbs. milk

Sauté pepper and onions in butter over low heat until softened. Add eggs and cook, stirring frequently. When eggs begin to "set" add cheese. Serve immediately when eggs are cooked to your liking. Supper for 2.

Beef with Four Peppers

This is an Americanized version of a dish we were served while honeymooning in Guadalajara. Since several of the peppers and spices weren't available locally, we let the produce market adjust the recipe.

2 lbs. sirloin steak, sliced into 2-inch strips
1-1/2 oz. fresh lime juice
Cracked black pepper

2 Tbs. oil
1 large onion, peeled and thinly sliced
3 cloves garlic, crushed through a press
1 fresh jalapeño, stemmed and minced
2 fresh serranos, stemmed and minced
1/2 bell pepper, diced
1 small Anaheim pepper, stemmed and diced
1 cup sliced fresh mushrooms
1 can beef broth
3/4 tsp. cumin
1 Tbs. cornstarch, mixed with 1-1/2 oz. cold water
1 Tbs. minced cilantro

Drizzle lime juice over meat, sprinkle with pepper, and set aside. In a large skillet with lid or in a wok, heat oil over medium high heat. Add garlic and onions, Cook for 3–4 minutes until soft but not browned. Remove from pan. Add peppers and mushrooms and cook for 4–5 minutes. Remove from pan and add to onion mixture. Add meat and juice to pan, browning the meat. Add peppers, onion, and mushrooms to pan. Pour in beef broth, add cumin, and simmer, covered, for 20 minutes. Add cornstarch and cook until thickened. Stir in cilantro just before serving. Serve with warm flour tortillas and cold beer.

Grilled Beef Tenderloin

2-1/2 lbs. tenderloin, trimmed
Black pepper
2 Tbs. oil
2 Tbs. butter

4 green onions, thinly sliced with tops
2 Tbs. parsley
1/4 cup brandy

Pepper meat liberally and rub in. Heat oil in large heavy skillet, preferably cast iron, over very high heat. Add tenderloin to pan. Sear for 2 minutes and turn for 2 minutes. Continue until all sides are seared. Using tongs, hold meat vertically to sear first on one end and then the other for 2 minutes on each end. Lay the meat down, reduce heat to medium and cook for 3 minutes, turn and cook for 3 minutes longer for each side (total of 12 minutes). Remove to cutting board and tent with foil. Add 2 Tbs. butter to skillet, when melted add green onions and parsley, and sauté for 3-4 minutes. Add brandy, bring to a boil, reduce heat, and simmer until reduced by half. Slice tenderloin, place on platter, and pour sauce over all. Serves 6-8.

Steaks and Chops á la Skillet

When either the weather, lack of time, or a bad case of procrastination has ruled out using the pit, you don't have to do without your steak. Use the same general guidelines as to thickness and cooking as found in "Grilling" (see Chapter One), the only difference being that you add the compound butter (i.e., Lemon Garlic, Lime Onion, or Soy Sauce Butter) after the steak is cooked.

Two ribeyes 1-1/4 to 1-1/2 inch thick (or clubs, sirloin strip, etc.)
2 Tbs. oil
Black pepper

Heat oil in a large heavy skillet, preferably cast iron, over high heat until nearly smoking. Pepper both sides of steak. Place steaks or chops in skillet and sear for 2 minutes. Turn meat with tongs and sear for 2 minutes. Reduce heat to medium, cooking for 3 additional minutes. Turn meat and cook for 2 additional minutes for medium rare. Serves 2.

Quail with Mushrooms

8 quail, halved, rinsed, and patted dry
16 large mushrooms, trimmed and sliced
3 green onions, thinly sliced with their tops
6 Tbs. unsalted butter
1/2 cup white wine
Black pepper

In a skillet large enough to hold half the quail, melt 2 Tbs. unsalted butter over medium high heat. Lightly pepper both sides of the quail and add to skillet without crowding, skin side down. Sauté for 5–6 minutes and turn. Cook 5–6 minutes more or until done. Remove to warm platter. If using one skillet, add 2 Tbs. more butter and repeat with remaining quail. Add remaining 2 Tbs. butter to skillet. When it has melted, add green onions and sauté for 2 minutes, add mushrooms, sauté for 2 more minutes and add wine. Simmer for 5–7 minutes. Pour sauce over quail and serve. Serves 4.

Sautéd Mushrooms

These go really well with any meat as a side dish, and they're available all year round.

16 large mushroom caps
1 clove garlic, crushed through a press
1 oz. brandy or sherry (different tastes, but they're both
    good)
3 Tbs. unsalted butter

Melt butter in a large skillet. When foam has subsided, add garlic. When garlic is fragrant, add mushrooms. Cook for 2–4 minutes, gently shaking the pan occasionally, until mushrooms start to color and give up their juices. Turn the mushrooms and add the brandy or sherry. Cook for 4–5 minutes longer. Take up the mushrooms with their juices and pass as a side dish for 4 people.

Cube Steaks and Coffee Gravy

You know cube steaks? That's those square tenderized unidentifiable chunks of meat that you buy when imagination has failed and nothing looks good. Actually, this gravy goes really well with any red meat. I first learned it at a hunting camp where the meat was venison.

1 lb. cube steaks
3 Tbs. oil
1 cup flour
1 Tbs. black pepper
1/2 cup coffee (leftover is fine)
Boiling water

Mix flour and pepper. Heat oil over medium high heat in a large skillet (as with frying). Dredge cube steaks in seasoned flour, shake off excess, and add to skillet. Brown meat, turn and brown other side. Remove to platter. Add 2–4 Tbs. of the seasoned flour (from the dredging) to skillet oil and brown flour. Add coffee and about 2 cups boiling water, stirring constantly. When gravy thickens, remove from heat and pour in a bowl. Serve with the meat. Serves 2.

Smothered Pork Chops

8 thin-sliced pork chops
1 large onion, peeled and sliced
Salt and pepper
Flour
Oil for cooking

In a large skillet with a lid, sear pork chops for one minute on each side in about 3 Tbs. oil. Remove and reserve. Using the technique for chicken-fried steak, make a thin gravy using water instead of milk. When gravy is made, return chops to the skillet, add onions, cover, and simmer for one hour. Serve with rice or mashed potatoes. Serves 4.

The Frank Fox Memorial Brunch (aka Sausage Gravy)

A great weekend breakfast. An all-time comfort food, it's also handy when you've got a herd to fix for, since you can cook as much as you need. Biscuits are required with this!

2 lbs. bulk sausage
Flour

Milk
Salt and pepper to taste

Break up sausage and brown in a large skillet over medium heat, then remove sausage with slotted spoon. Make gravy as directed with chicken-fried steak. When thin gravy is made, return sausage to pan and heat until gravy is thick. Add salt and pepper to taste. Serve over biscuits. A one-dish meal! Serves 6–8 . . . or Frank and 3 others.

Oysters on Toast

16 oysters, shucked
1 Tbs. butter
1 green onion, thinly sliced with tops
1 can beef consommé
1 Tbs. Worcestershire sauce
4 slices bread, toasted, crusts removed
1 Tbs. minced parsley tops

In a small skillet, just large enough to hold the oysters in one layer, melt the butter over medium heat. Add green onions and cook for 2–3 minutes. Add consommé and Worcestershire. Bring to a boil, reduce heat, and simmer. Add oysters and simmer gently until edges of oysters just start to curl. Cut each piece of toast diagonally into quarters. Place 4 toast points on each of four serving plates. Top each point with an oyster and a little of the broth. Sprinkle with parsley. Appetizers for 4.

Tex-Mex Tacos

2 Tbs. oil
2 lbs. ground beef
1 onion, chopped
2 cloves garlic, minced
1 Tbs. chili powder
1/2 Tbs. ground cumin
1/8 tsp. cayenne
1 cup chopped lettuce
2 large tomatoes, chopped
1 cup grated cheese
Pepper Patch Picante Sauce (see recipe in Chapter Four)
Warm flour tortillas or corn tortillas crisped in hot oil

Heat oil in a large skillet over medium heat. Add onion and garlic, and sauté for 3–4 minutes or until softened and fragrant. Break up meat into skillet and brown thoroughly. Add chili powder, cumin, and cayenne, and reduce heat. Simmer for 10 minutes. Drain. Set meat in a bowl in the center of the table with the tomatoes, cheese, lettuce, etc., and let everybody build their own. If you're wanting crispy corn taco shells, heat 1 inch oil in an 8-inch skillet. Place 1 corn tortilla in the hot oil for 20 seconds. Turn, fold in half and cook for 20–30 seconds on each side. Repeat with remaining tortillas.

Larry's Blackened Fish

In an area that is virtually overrun with good cooks, Larry is one of the best. He is also the author of a lasagna recipe, which he won't divulge, that has wrecked more than one diet.

SEASONING MIX:
1-1/2 Tbs. sweet paprika
2 tsp. salt
1 tsp. onion powder
1 tsp. garlic powder
1 tsp. cayenne
3/4 tsp. black pepper
3/4 tsp. white pepper
1/2 tsp. dried oregano
1/2 tsp. dried thyme
Six 8–10 oz. fish filets, cut 1/2 inch thick
3 sticks unsalted butter, melted in small skillet

Heat large cast iron skillet over very high heat until it is beyond the smoking stage (it cannot get too hot), at least 10 minutes. Thoroughly combine the seasoning ingredients. Place in shaker-type bottle if possible. Dip each filet in melted butter so that both sides are well coated. Sprinkle seasoning mix generously and evenly on both sides of filets, patting it in by hand. Place in the hot skillet and pour 1 tsp. of melted butter on top (careful of flame-up). Cook uncovered until it looks charred, 2 minutes, turn and repeat butter, cook until done, about 2 minutes. *Repeat* with remaining filets, serve piping hot. Makes 6 servings.

Compliments of Larry Burruss, San Marcos, Texas

Chapter Four
Other Good Stuff
─────── *STARTERS* ───────

Caviar Pie

Nancy gave me this recipe six or eight years ago, and I have never failed to get a boat load of compliments on it. There are certain folks, who shall remain anonymous, that seem to just camp by the caviar pie all night.

> Three 8-oz. pkgs. cream cheese at room temperature
> One 8-oz. carton sour cream
> 1 Tbs. mayonnaise
> Juice of 2 lemons
> 3 hard-boiled eggs, minced
> 1 medium onion, very finely minced
> 2 3-oz. jars of black caviar (the cheap kind)

Combine first four ingredients in a medium bowl and mix until smooth. Spread half of mixture in the bottom of a 10 inch glass pie pan. Evenly sprinkle onion over first layer and then sprinkle the minced eggs over the onions. Spread remaining cheese mixture over the hard-cooked eggs, and "ice the pie" with the caviar. Serve with unsalted crackers as a winning hors d'oeuvre.

Courtesy of Nancy Becker, Houston

Cool-as-a-Cucumber Soup

3 large cucumbers
2 large cloves garlic, peeled and crushed through a press
1-1/2 tsp. salt
2 tsp. dried dill
2 Tbs. chopped chives
2 Tbs. lemon juice
1 pint sour cream
1 pint half-and-half
Milk
Black pepper

Peel and seed cucumbers. Puree in a food processor and add garlic, salt, lemon juice, dill, and chives. Pulse to blend. In a large bowl combine the pureed mixture, half-and-half, sour cream, and milk enough to give you the consistency of a thick cream soup. Chill for at least four hours before serving. Top each serving with a couple of grinds of fresh pepper. Serves a dozen.

Eggs Diablo

6 hard-boiled eggs
1 tsp. finely-minced onions
Mayonnaise
Mrs. Dash

Peel the hard-boiled eggs and cut them into halves lengthwise. Remove the egg yolks and mix them with enough mayonnaise to give a creamy texture that will still hold its shape. Add the onions and Mrs. Dash to taste. Refill the little holes in the eggs with the yolk mixture, cover, and chill. Garnish with paprika or cayenne before serving. Serves 6.

Hot Potato and Greens Salad

Here's a twist on the hot potato salad that will put a lot of gold stars in your column.

    6-8 strips bacon, fried crisp
    3 medium potatoes, peeled and cubed
    1 small onion, coarsely chopped
    4 cups bitter greens (endive, chicory, etc.) washed and torn
        into bite-sized pieces
    Salt and pepper to taste

Place potatoes in a small pan, cover with water, bring to boil, and cook until very tender. Remove from heat and reserve (do not drain). In a large non-reactive skillet, fry bacon until crisp. Remove from skillet, drain, and reserve. Drain potatoes, reserving cooking liquid. Mash potatoes, adding cooking liquid until the potatoes are the consistency of mayonnaise. Heat 1–2 Tbs. bacon drippings in the skillet until hot. Add greens and stir constantly until just wilted. Put greens and onion into large bowl, adding hot potatoes and toss. Garnish with bacon and serve. Serves 4–6.

Fiesta Salad

2 bunches radishes, trimmed, halved, and thinly sliced
1 bunch green onions, trimmed and thinly sliced (include
    tops)
1/2 medium bell pepper, finely chopped
Two 16-oz. cartons small-curd cottage cheese, drained
1 cup mayonnaise
1 Tbs. dried dill, or more to taste
Salt and pepper to taste

Combine all the ingredients and chill for two hours before serving. Serve on lettuce leaves.

Alternative: Combine as above and puree in a food processor to use as a dip; especially good with crudités.

German Paté

Not a true paté (I'm too lazy to do all that work), but quite different. You'll either like it or not. No middle ground here.

1-1/2 lbs. braunschweiger sausage
One 8-oz. carton sour cream
1/3 cup mayonnaise (approximate)
3/4 cup finely-minced onion
1-1/2 Tbs. prepared horseradish

Combine all the ingredients in a bowl and mix thoroughly. Press mixture into a loaf pan or a decorative mold. Chill for three to four hours. Unmold and serve with cocktail rye and hot

German mustard on the side. This makes a good party hors d'oeuvre.

Note: Make sure you line your mold with plastic wrap as this does not unmold willingly. You don't want to lightly oil the mold because it will set up on the paté and give it a "funky" taste.

Guacamole

Great stuff—it's a dip, a garnish, a side dish, or a salad. Everybody does this their own way, but this one is quite reliable.

    3 fully ripe avocados, peeled, seeded, and mashed
    3/4 tsp. garlic powder
    Juice of one lime
    2 Tbs. salsa picante
    Salt and pepper to taste
    Tabasco sauce to taste

Combine all ingredients in a non-reactive bowl, sprinkle additional lime juice over the surface to prevent discoloration. Cover and refrigerate for up to several hours before serving.

Pico de Gallo

Goes well with fajitas, brisket, tostados as a dip, scrambled eggs, omelettes, and lots of other good stuff.

    3-4 large ripe tomatoes, chopped
    1 large onion, minced

2-3 fresh jalapeños, minced
2-3 fresh serrano peppers, minced
3 Tbs. minced fresh cilantro
2-3 cloves garlic, crushed
1 tsp. cumin
Juice of 1-2 Mexican limes (small, cheap kind)

Mix everything together except the cilantro and lime juice. Refrigerate in a non-reactive, covered container for four hours before serving. Remove from refrigerator and stir in the cilantro and lime juice just before serving.

Shrimp Avocado Cocktail

1 onion, peeled, thinly sliced and separated into rings
2 cloves garlic, peeled and crushed through a press
1 fresh jalapeño, finely minced (with seeds)
1 cup lime juice (fresh squeezed, if possible)
1 lb. medium shrimp, peeled and deveined
3 avocados, peeled and cut into 1/2 inch cubes
1 Tbs. minced cilantro

Combine the first four ingredients in a small, non-reactive saucepan. Bring to a boil and immediately remove from heat. In a glass pie pan, scatter out the shrimp. Pour the hot marinade over the shrimp, cover, and cool to room temperature. Refrigerate for 5 hours. One hour before serving, toss avocado cubes with shrimp. Using a slotted spoon, divide the mixture into 6 cocktail dishes. Top with a bit of cilantro and serve.

Tortilla Whirls

One 8-oz. pkg. cream cheese, room temperature
1/2 cup minced ripe olives, drained
1/4 cup minced canned jalapeños, drained
6 flour tortillas

Combine cream cheese with olives and jalapeños thoroughly, and allow to rest for an hour or so. Spread each tortilla generously with mixture and roll up. Slice tortilla rolls 3/8 inch thick and arrange on a serving tray. Any leftover filling can be used for stuffing celery . . . or stuffing a baked potato another day.

Peppy Melon Cocktail

This is where you finally get to use that melon baller that somebody gave you at a wedding shower.

2 cups watermelon, seeded, cut into balls with melon baller
2 cups cantaloupe, same way
2 cups honeydew melon, same way
2 cups strawberries, rinsed and hulled
1 Tbs. coarse black pepper

Combine everything, toss, cover, and refrigerate until serving. Serves 8–10, looks real pretty, and packs a little surprise.

Quickie Salad Dressing

6 Tbs. olive oil
2 Tbs. tarragon vinegar
1/2 Tbs. freshly ground black pepper
1/2 tsp. garlic powder
2 Tbs. ground Parmesan cheese

Combine all ingredients in a jar, and shake vigorously. Refrigerate for at least two hours to allow the flavors to blend. Serve over any type of green salad.

ENTREES

Burrocks

We are not sure about the spelling of the name of this recipe, as it has been handed down a couple of generations. You can double the recipe and then reheat in the microwave. They are also good at room temperature for use in lunch boxes.

Any good yeast roll recipe
1 lb. lean ground beef
1 medium onion, chopped
1/2 small head of cabbage, shredded
Salt and pepper to taste

Brown ground meat and onions together in a large skillet. When the meat is cooked, pour off any liquids and add the finely-shredded cabbage. Cover and cook slowly over low heat until

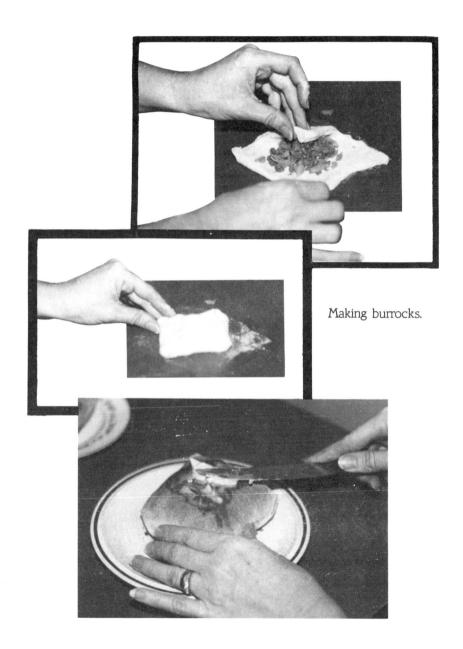

Making burrocks.

the cabbage is tender. Drain the mixture in a colander and cool. Meanwhile, prepare the yeast roll recipe. After the dough has risen the first time, punch it down and roll out the dough until it is about 1/4 inch thick. Cut into 3 to 4 inch squares. Put about 1-2 tablespoons of the cooled cabbage mixture in the center of each dough square. Fold over and seal. When the cabbage-stuffed rolls have risen for the second time, bake until golden brown. Serve hot with butter.

Note: The object here is to plan ahead and have the cabbage mixture cooked and cooled to coincide with the end of the first rising of the hot rolls. The cabbage can be cooked ahead of time and refrigerated, as it does take about 1-2 hours to cool down, depending on the weather, etc.

Cheese Enchiladas

2 Tbs. oil
2 Tbs. flour
2 tsp. garlic powder
1 Tbs. cumin
3 Tbs. red chili powder
Boiling water
1 dozen corn tortillas
1 medium onion, chopped
4 cups grated longhorn cheese
Oil

In a large skillet brown 2 Tbs. flour in 2 Tbs. oil until *dark* brown, almost burned. Add the garlic powder, cumin, and chili powder and stir until frothy. Slowly add about two cups of boiling water and cook until slightly thick. Keep this mixture hot in the skillet. In the meanwhile, heat approximately 1/2 inch oil in another large skillet until almost hot enough to smoke. Using tongs, dip the corn tortillas one at a time through the hot oil very quickly and then through the hot red sauce. Roll about 2-3 Tbs. grated cheese and 1/2 tsp. of grated onion into each tortilla. Stack in a baking dish and then repeat with another tortilla. If the red sauce starts to get thick, thin it with a little more boiling water. Pour remaining hot sauce over stacked tortillas and sprinkle with onion and cheese. Cover with foil and bake in 350° oven until cheese has melted. Serves 4-6.

Note: The amount of cheese and onions used is according to your own taste. If you like lots of either, increase the amount used in this recipe.

Enchiladas II

If you're going to take the time and trouble to make a proper pot of chili, the chances are that you'll make more than will be eaten at one sitting. No problem, it freezes beautifully. When you're wondering "What's for supper?" and find the frozen chili, here's a great one-dish meal.

    1-1/2 quarts chili
    1 large onion, minced
    2-3 cups longhorn cheese, grated
    10-12 corn tortillas
    Cooking oil

Heat about 1/4–1/2 inch oil in a small skillet until almost smoking. Using tongs, quickly plunge each tortilla in the hot oil for 3–4 seconds and place a layer of tortillas in a shallow baking dish. Layer on a generous amount of chili, then onion, then cheese. Repeat with another layer of tortillas, chili, onions, and cheese. Repeat until all tortillas are used, ending with a generous coating of cheese. Cover and cook for about 20–25 minutes in a 350° oven. Crack open a cold beer and go for it. Serves 4–6.

Disguised Leftovers

This is a favorite of our daughter, Leslie. She always wanted pot roast so that she could have the leftovers this way. In fact, if she could skip the original pot roast and go straight to the disguised leftovers, she would.

    2 cups leftover pot roast, cut into cubes
    1 cup leftover roast gravy
    Leftover cooked carrots and potatoes
    1 biscuit recipe

Cut the leftover meat and vegetables into small cubes, mix with the gravy, and place in a 4-quart baking dish. If you do not have enough gravy to go around, you can substitute beef broth. Place biscuits on top of the meat and cook in a 350° oven until biscuits are done . . . about 20–25 minutes. It takes a little longer than usual because the biscuits are resting on liquid rather than a cookie sheet.

Note: The shallower the baking dish, the faster the biscuits cook. Also, frozen green peas or broccoli are excellent additions to the potatoes and carrots.

Ham and Scalloped Potatoes

This is a great way to use leftover Christmas ham. If you don't have leftovers, buy smoked ham slices.

2 cups diced cooked ham
4 large white potatoes, peeled and thinly sliced
1/2 cup diced onion
2 cups thin white sauce

To make white sauce, cook 2 Tbs. flour in 2 Tbs. butter until done, but not brown. Add 2 cups milk and cook until slightly thickened. Layer potatoes, onions, and ham in baking dish. Add white sauce to cover the potatoes and ham. If you don't have quite enough white sauce (depending upon the size of baking dish), add milk to cover. Cover and bake until potatoes are tender, 30–45 minutes. Uncover for the last 10 minutes to brown top.

Note: This is what our kids refer to as "Mom Food" (good basic home-cooking, like you remember your mom cooking).

Light Tasty Chicken

6 Tbs. olive oil
Juice of 1-1/2 large juicy limes
3 large green onions, finely chopped, with the tops
3 large cloves garlic, minced
1-1/2 Tbs. fresh ground black pepper
One 3-lb. chicken, rinsed and quartered

Combine oil, lime juice, onions, garlic, and pepper in a small saucepan, and cook covered over low heat until the onions are softened. Place chicken quarters in a baking dish, pour onion mixture over chicken, cover, and bake at 350° for 1 hour. Serves 4.

─────── *PASTA* ───────

All of the recipes in this section are suitable for either fresh or dried pastas. Obviously, homemade is better. In fact, that's all we use. When you buy your pasta machine, it'll have a good recipe with it—use it. That's basically the same one we're using.

Most of these recipes were developed to make use of goodies available locally. Most pasta sauce recipes are written by people in the East, particularly New York City, and they assume you can just zip out to the corner Italian deli and pick up a few specialized ingredients. Our nearest reliable source is a scant 240 miles up the Interstate, hence the improvisation.

Fettucini Alfredo

1 lb. fettucini, cooked al dente and drained
1 cup heavy cream at room temperature
2 oz. white wine
1 stick unsalted butter, in thin slices
3/4 bunch parsley tops, minced
5 small green onions, thinly sliced (include tops)
3 cloves garlic, crushed
1/2 Tbs. oregano (fresh dried leaves, if possible)
3/4 cup Parmesan cheese

Put the hot pasta in a large, warmed, ceramic bowl. Add the butter and cheese and toss constantly. The heat of the pasta should melt the butter and cheese. Add the parsley, onions, garlic, oregano, and wine, and continue tossing. Add the cream, 1/4 cup at a time, until the sauce reaches desired consistency. Serve immediately. Serves 6-8.

Pasta Vinaigrette

2 Tbs. olive oil
2/3 cup red onion, chopped
2/3 cup red bell pepper, chopped
2/3 cup green bell pepper, chopped
3 cloves garlic, crushed through a press
1 Tbs. oregano
1/2 cup chopped fresh basil leaves
1 tsp. black pepper
1 tsp. crushed hot red pepper
1/4 tsp. salt
1/4 cup olive oil
5 Tbs. white wine vinegar
Parmesan or Romano cheese, grated

Heat oil over medium high heat in a large skillet. Add onions, garlic, red and green bell pepper, garlic, and oregano. Sauté together for 6-8 minutes. Add basil, red and black pepper, salt, olive oil, and vinegar. Simmer for 10 minutes. Turn off heat, cover, and let soak together for 1 hours. Pour over pasta cooked al dente and toss. Pass cheese separately.

Pasta con Pollo

We usually have some cold grilled chicken meat in the 'fridge. (No sense wasting grill space!) However, if you're going from scratch on this one, we've included a quickie that works just fine.

    1 lb. pasta recipe (fetticuni is our first choice) cooked al
        dente and drained
    4 grilled chicken breasts, sliced thin
    3 Tbs. olive oil
    1 red onion, thinly sliced
    3 cloves garlic, minced
    8 oz. fresh mushrooms, thinly sliced
    2 Tbs. white wine
    1 bell pepper, thinly sliced
    2 Tbs. parsley, minced
    1 tsp. crushed red pepper

Heat oil in a medium skillet over medium heat. Add onion, garlic, and bell pepper; reduce heat to low; cover and cook for about 10 minutes or until softened. Increase heat to medium high and add mushrooms, wine, and red pepper; cook for about five minutes. Add chicken and parsley and cover; reduce heat to medium and simmer for five more minutes. Toss with hot pasta in a warm ceramic bowl.

Note: If you don't have any grilled chicken breasts available, here's how you do it. When you first get home pour one bottle of Italian salad dressing over 4 boneless, skinless chicken breasts. An hour later, grill the breasts 4 inches from the heat in the oven broiler for 4 minutes per side, or until well browned on each side.

Pasta from the Gulf

2 Tbs. unsalted butter
2 Tbs. flour
1 cup milk
1 cup Baby Swiss cheese, grated
1/4 tsp. cayenne
2 oz. white wine
1-1/2 lb. medium shrimp, boiled, deveined, peeled and split
    lengthwise
2 Tbs. minced parsley
1 lb. pasta, cooked al dente

Melt butter in a medium saucepan over low heat. Stir in flour and cook, stirring constantly, until smooth. Remove from heat and add milk. Return to heat, increase heat to boiling, stirring constantly. When sauce boils, add cheese, cayenne, and wine. Continue to stir until cheese melts. Add shrimp and heat until shrimp are hot (about 1-2 minutes). Pour over pasta and top with parsley. Serves 4.

Note: If shrimp are unavailable, two large lobster tails work famously.

Pasta Brasada

We came up with this one when everything in the garden got ripe at the same time. Vary the mix to suit yourself.

6-8 large cloves garlic, crushed through a press
4 Tbs. olive oil

6-7 green onions, thinly chopped with their tops
2 fresh green cayenne peppers, stemmed and chopped
1 fresh jalapeño. stemmed and chopped
1 fresh serrano, stemmed and chopped
1-1/2 cups diced red sweet peppers
1/2 cup fresh basil leaves, chopped
1/4 cup fresh oregano, chopped
1/2 Tbs. cumin
4-5 medium tomatoes, peeled and chopped
1 Tbs. tarragon vinegar
1/4 cup minced parsley
1 lb. fresh pasta, cooked al dente
Parmesan or Romano cheese

Heat oil in a skillet and add garlic. Cook for 1 minute. Add onions and peppers and cook an additional two minutes. Add basil, oregano, tomatoes, cumin, parsley, and vinegar. Bring to a boil; reduce heat and simmer for about 10 minutes, until juicy. Pour over pasta and toss. Pass cheese at the table. Serves 4.

Hill Country Ravioli in Southwestern Sauce

Talk about a conglomeration of ethnic background! Strange as it may sound, when everything goes together, it really works. The New Mexico Red Puree takes about an hour to make, so plan accordingly.

Ravioli Filling:

> 1 lb. finely ground venison
> 1/2 medium onion, finely minced
> 3 cloves garlic, crushed through a press
> 1 serrano pepper, stemmed and minced
> 3 Tbs. olive oil
> 4 oz. Mozzarella cheese, shredded

Heat olive oil in a medium skillet. Add onion, garlic, and pepper and sauté for one minute. Add venison and brown thoroughly, breaking up the meat into small pieces. Drain and place in a bowl. Stir in the cheese.

Pasta:

One recipe pasta, rolled out to 1/8 inch thickness, and cut into 3 inch by 4 inch rectangle.

To fill:

Starting at one narrow end of each rectangle place 1–2 tablespoons of filling on each rectangle Moisten the edges of the pasta with a little water, fold over and seal edges.

To cook:

Place a few ravioli at a time in a pot of barely boiling water and cook about two minutes. Drain and remove to a baking dish. Repeat until all ravioli are cooked.

Sauce:

> 1/2 cup onions, chopped
> 3 cloves garlic, minced

2/3 cup New Mexico Red Pepper Puree
1 8-oz. can tomato sauce
1/2 Tbs. cumin
1/2 lb. Monterey Jack cheese, shredded

Cook onions and garlic in about 2 Tbs. oil, covered, over low heat for about ten minutes or until softened but not browned. Add pepper puree, tomato sauce, and cumin, and simmer for 15 minutes.

To make pepper puree:

Stem, seed, and chop 20 dried New Mexico red peppers (dried Anaheim peppers, available from several of the mail order houses listed in Appendix or at any roadside stand in the Southwest). Place in a small non-reactive saucepan, cover with water, bring to a boil, cover, reduce heat to low for 30 minutes. Strain, reserving liquid. Puree in a food processor adding enough reserved cooking liquid to reach the consistency of tomato sauce. Press through a fine sieve, and there you have the ultimate in pure pepper essence.

Getting It Together:

Place ravioli in a single crowded layer in a shallow baking dish. Pour sauce over ravioli, and scatter cheese generously on top. Bake at 350° until cheese melts. Serves four generously.

GRAZING THROUGH THE GARDEN

ABOUT HERBS

Throughout this book you'll notice that we use an awful lot of the same herbs. The reason is simple—in line with the theme of this book: They are readily available. Sporadically available through the year at the grocery store, they are always available fresh, either from the garden, or from the potted plants on the patio.

Herb gardening is not rocket science . . . if I can do it, anybody can. No vast acreage or equipment is required, either. Our herb patch is 6 feet by 14 feet, and includes sweet basil, lemon basil, rosemary, dill, oregano, and thyme. We don't raise cilantro, garlic, or parsley because we have a reliable year-round supply available at the store and they are cheap.

All you really need is a patch of ground that gets good sunlight, a few bags of composted manure from the discount store, and an afternoon to work the ground into shape. After the ground is worked, mix in the manure, smooth over, and plant your herbs. We prefer to use the bedding-size plants, rather than start from seed—we're into instant gratification! Water when they need it, and enjoy. The herb garden keeps giving until the first killing frost.

When you plant your garden, put a couple of plants of each herb in a large clay pot for winter use. Harvest and dry your garden in the fall. Once you've experienced fresh herbs, nothing else will be the same.

Natha Lee's Coleslaw

4 cups shredded cabbage
1 cup shredded carrots
1 cup mayonnaise (not salad dressing)
2 Tbs. sugar
2 Tbs. tarragon vinegar
1/2 tsp. celery seeds

Mix mayonnaise, sugar, tarragon vinegar, and celery seeds together. Mix with the cabbage and carrots to taste and serve immediately.

Note: The dressing can be made ahead and kept in the refrigerator for several days. Do not put it on the slaw until ready to serve.

Artichokes with Basil Butter

As an appetizer, figure one artichoke for every two persons.

2 artichokes, bottom trimmed and sharp leaf points
     removed
1-1/2 sticks butter, melted
1/4 cup fresh basil leaves, minced
1 Tbs. lime juice

Combine hot melted butter, lime juice, and basil leaves. Allow to rest. Steam artichokes in a covered vessel for about 45 minutes or until done (the leaves will come off easily). Place each artichoke convenient to two people. Reheat butter and pass as a dip.

Cabbage Steamed in Chicken Broth

New Year's Day Special!

1 medium head cabbage, cored and quartered
Two 13-3/4 oz. cans chicken broth
1 onion, peeled and thickly sliced
Black pepper to taste

Place onions in bottom of a large 4-quart pot. Place cabbage on top. Pour chicken broth over all and bring to a boil. Reduce heat, cover, and simmer for 15 minutes or until tender. Season with black pepper. Serves 4–6.

Creamed Corn

6–8 ears fresh corn
3 Tbs. butter
Half-and-half
Salt and pepper to taste

Using a very sharp knife, cut the kernels of corn from the cob. Scrape the cob and add the pulp and juice to the kernels in the pot. Cook with butter and small amount of water until tender. Add 1/4 cup half-and-half (or milk), and cook over low heat until reduced and thick. Salt and pepper to taste.

Tomatoes, Onions, and Basil

A super summer salad; the key here is everything must be as *fresh* as possible.

  3 very large beefsteak-type tomatoes, preferably home
       grown
  1/2 large sweet onion (Texas 1015, Vidalia, Walla Walla),
       sliced paper thin
  1/2 cup fresh basil leaves, chopped
  1 clove garlic, mashed
  1/3 cup olive oil

Put garlic in a jar with the olive oil. Add basil, cover tightly, shake, and set aside for a half hour or so. Slice tomatoes 3/8 inch thick. On a serving plate, alternate tomatoes and onion slices. Pour basil oil over all, discarding garlic. Top with a few grinds of black pepper.

Summer Squash Pot

  3 large yellow squash
  1 medium zucchini
  1 medium onion, chopped
  1/2 cup chopped sweet red pepper
  2 Tbs. unsalted butter

Melt butter in a 3-quart saucepan. Add onions and cook covered until softened. Add peppers, squash, and 1/4 cup of water. Cook over medium heat until tender. Serves 4.

Pepper Patch Picante

I go through the pepper patch once a week or so and pick everything that's ready to be picked. Then I find a jar that'll hold 'em and make up the sauce. Here's the recipe for this week's 8-oz. jar. This is not a preserve. I don't know how long it'll keep because we eat it on everything—beans, roast, peas, greens, sandwiches—whatever!

1 Tbs. chili pequins (very hot, tiny)
6 medium Thai peppers (very hot, very small), or more chili pequins
8 red sweet peppers (mild, medium sized, a little longer than a jalapeño)
2 banana peppers (mild)
1 jalapeño (hot)
2 green cayennes (hot)
2 serranos (hot)
2 cloves garlic
1 Tbs. onion, minced
1/2 cup cider vinegar

Remove stems from the peppers and chop them. Blanch for 1 minute in boiling water, drain, and rinse with cold water. Put garlic and onion in a clean jar and fill with the peppers. Cover with boiling vinegar, seal, and store in the fridge for a week. Open the jar and enjoy.

Spicy Cranberry Relish

Here's a little goody that will add spice to your next ham, smoked turkey, or roast!

2 cups cranberries (fresh)
1 cup sugar
1 fresh orange, peeled, sectioned, and diced
1 fresh jalapeño, stemmed, seeded, and minced
1 cup water
1 Tbs. minced cilantro

Combine all ingredients except the cilantro in a non-reactive saucepan and bring to a boil. Reduce heat, and simmer covered until berries begin to pop. Strain and "bump" in a food processor until a coarse "jam" consistency. Chill for an hour. Stir in cilantro just before serving.

——————— *FINISHERS* ———————

If you have done everything else right, then a dessert should be simple and straightforward, preferably on the light side. We do an awful lot of cheese and fresh fruit at our house. However, here are some ideas that nobody has complained about yet.

Lazy Man's Ice Cream

6 eggs
2-1/2 cups sugar
3 pints heavy cream

    2 tsp. vanilla
    1/2 tsp. salt
    Milk

Beat eggs, gradually adding sugar until mixture thickens. Add remaining ingredients, except the milk. Mix thoroughly. Pour into ice cream freezer, and add milk to the "fill line." Freeze according to manufacturer's instruction. Makes a gallon.

Coffee and Kahlua Ice Cream

    Make ice cream as above, but add 2 oz. Kahlua and 2 Tbs. instant coffee which had been dissolved in 1/4 cup water before you add the milk. Freeze as above.

Hill Country Peach Ice Cream

    Make ice cream as above, adding 2 cups of fresh peaches that have been peeled, diced, sugared lightly, and chilled, before adding milk. If peaches don't have good "peachy taste", try adding 1/4 cup of Peach Schnapps. Freeze as above.

Strawberry Ice Cream

    Wash and hull 1–2 pints of strawberries. Quarter each berry, sprinkle with 1–1/2 Tbs. Kirschwasser and 1 Tbs. sugar. Allow to macerate for a couple of hours, then add to the basic ice cream above, before milk is added. Freeze as above.

Brown Cake with Tan Icing

I've got no idea where this recipe came from, but it was old when I was born, so that'll give you some idea! It was one of my mother's recipes, and I suspect that she got it from her mother, based on the condition of the original card. Still tastes good though. When birthday time rolls around, this is my personal preference.

    1 cup shortening
    2 cups brown sugar
    2 eggs
    1 cup cold coffee
    3 cups flour
    1 tsp. baking powder
    3/4 tsp. soda
    1 tsp. cloves
    1 tsp. cinnamon
    1 tsp. nutmeg
    1 cup raisins

Mix in the usual way and pour into a greased loaf tin. Bake in a moderate oven (350°) for about 45 minutes. Cover thickly with mocha frosting.

Mocha Frosting:
Cream 1-1/2 Tbs. butter, blend in 1/2 Tbs. powdered cocoa and 1/2 cup powdered sugar. When thick, add alternately 2-1/2 Tbs.

strong, strained coffee, 1 Tbs. thick cream, and about one cup more of powdered sugar . . . enough to make it spread. Add 1 tsp. vanilla.

Peach Cobbler

The best cobblers are made out of fresh fruit, of course. However, if you are unable to obtain fresh, frozen is a good substitute.

1/2–3/4 cup sugar
1 Tbs. flour
4 cups fresh peaches, peeled and sliced
3 Tbs. butter or margarine
1 cup flour
2 Tbs. sugar
1-1/2 tsp. baking powder
1/2 tsp. salt
3 Tbs. shortening
1/3 cup milk
1 egg, beaten

Heat oven to 400°. Put sliced peaches in a 2-quart baking dish. Mix sugar and 1 Tbs. flour together and sprinkle over the peaches. Cut butter into small pieces and arrange over top of fruit mixture. Heat fruit mixture in oven until hot. Mix together 1 cup flour, 2 Tbs. sugar, baking powder, and salt. Cut in shortening until mixture has consistency of meal. Add milk and beaten egg. Drop by small spoonfuls over the hot fruit and bake 20–25 minutes or until topping is golden brown. Serve warm and, if desired, with cream. Umm good!

Note: The amount of sugar used is determined by the ripeness of the fruit. The riper it is, the less sugar you use. If you drop the topping by large spoonfuls, the dough in the center will not get done by the time the topping is brown.

Pecan Pie

Pastry for 9-inch pie
3 eggs
2/3 cup sugar
1/2 tsp. salt
1/3 cup butter or margarine, melted
1 cup dark corn syrup
1 cup pecans, either halves or broken pieces

Heat oven to 375°. Prepare pastry for 9-inch pie. Beat together eggs, sugar, salt, butter, and syrup. Add nuts, pour into pastry-lined pie pan. Bake 40–50 minutes or until set.

Note: Pecan halves make a fancier pie but it is easier to slice if you use pieces. Pie is set when a sharp knife blade inserted into center of pie comes out clean.

Pastry for 8- or 9-Inch Pie

1 cup flour
1/2 tsp. salt
1/3 cup plus 1 Tbs. shortening
2–4 Tbs. ice water

Mix flour and salt in a bowl. Cut in shortening until the mixture is the consistency of meal. Sprinkle in the cold water, 1 Tbs. at a time, mixing until the flour is all moistened and dough cleans side of the bowl. Gather the dough into a ball. Shape on lightly floured board with rolling pin. Dough should be about 2 inches larger than the pie pan when it is inverted. Fold into quarters and ease into your pie pan.

Note: If your shortening is cold it works better, and always use *cold* water.

Strawberry Shortcake

Strawberries are one of the great seasonal blessing of our area, being available fresh about eight months of the year. The cake you use for the base is less important than using fresh berries, and is purely a matter of choice. Some folks like angel food cake, some like a biscuit type, and some (including yours truly) lean toward pound cake. I would have included my pound cake recipe, but since it starts out with a pound of flour, a pound of sugar, a pound of butter, and a dozen eggs, I figured that I'd just save ya'll the time it takes to write those letters chastising me for lousing up your nice healthy diet. So here's the fruit and toppings—put it on whatever you want.

    3 cups fresh strawberries, washed, hulled, and halved
        lengthwise
    1 Tbs. sugar
    2 oz. Grand Marnier

1 pint whipping cream
1 Tbs. sugar

Sprinkle 1 Tbs. sugar over strawberries and follow with the Grand Marnier (or any other orange-flavored liqueur). Toss to coat. Allow to set for about 2 hours at room temperature. Just before serving, beat the cream until very thick in a chilled bowl, adding sugar slowly. For each serving, place about 1/4 cup berries on the cake, layer on a couple Tbs. of whipped cream, add some more berries, another layer of cream, and then drizzle the top with some of the juice that's collected in the berry bowl. Serves 6. If you choose to take the lazy way out, you can substitute vanilla ice cream for the whipped cream, without loss of calories!

Sweet Potato Pie

Pastry for 9-inch pie
2 eggs
2 cups cooked and mashed sweet potatoes
3/4 cup sugar
1 tsp. cinnamon
1/4 tsp. cloves
1/4 tsp. nutmeg
1-2/3 cup evaporated milk

Heat oven to 425°. Prepare pie pastry and bake for 15 minutes. Mix all other ingredients in a medium saucepan and cook over medium heat until mixture starts to thicken. Pour into partially baked pie crust, reduce oven heat to 350°, and bake about 30 minutes longer or until knife inserted in center comes out clean. Cool. Serve plain or with whipped cream.

Note: Find sweet potatoes that are all about the same size so they will cook evenly. Scrub them and place whole in a large covered Dutch oven. Cover with water and simmer until done. Peel and mash. You may have to remove some "strings" in order to make a smooth mixture. This recipe also makes wonderful pumpkin pie. Just substitute a one-pound can of pumpkin for the sweet potatoes.

——————— BREADS ———————

Buttermilk Biscuits

This is another of the basics. Another tip of the black felt hat to Natha, author of this particular blessing. We've several friends who have repeatedly make true oinkers of themselves when she fires up the oven. Once again, good biscuits are not a deep mystery, they just require learning a couple of simple techniques. These techniques are the difference between a flakey pleasure and a small cannonball.

  2 cups flour
  2 tsp. sugar
  2 tsp. baking powder
  1 tsp. salt
  1/2 tsp. soda
  1/3 cup shortening
  2/3 cup buttermilk

Sift baking powder, sugar, salt, soda, and flour into bowl. Cut in the shortening until the mixture is the consistency of meal. Add the buttermilk and stir just until the dough is soft and pliable.

Don't overmix or the biscuits will be tough. Turn out onto a floured surface and knead lightly about 20–25 times. Roll out dough to about 1/2 inch thick. Cut with biscuit cutter. Cook in a hot oven (450°) on an ungreased baking sheet for about 10–12 minutes.

Notes: If dough is not pliable, add a little more milk, but be careful—too much milk makes a sticky dough. If you want crusty sides on your biscuits, cook them about 1 inch apart on a cookie sheet. If you want soft sides, cook them close together in a pie pan with their sides touching. Your oven must be *hot* when you put in the biscuits or they won't rise well and will not be as fluffy and tender.

Cornbread

All right, pay attention! This is serious stuff! Basic, even! You could cook this in *any* kind of pan, but if you want to get that extra great cornbread that you've seen pictures of, then cast iron is the way, the truth, and the *only* answer! My particular choice for a single recipe is an 8-inch cast-iron skillet that has been around since they made dirt. Melt your shortening in the skillet. That way, the pan is lightly greased and preheated. Since cornbread is the only thing cooked in this particular skillet, clean-up amounts to a good wipe out with a dry paper towel.

1 cup yellow cornmeal
1 cup flour
4 tsp. baking powder
1 tsp. sugar

3/4 tsp. salt
1/4 cup shortening, melted
1 egg
1 cup milk

Combine first five ingredients in a mixing bowl and blend thoroughly. Beat egg and milk together and add to dry ingredients. Mix quickly and thoroughly. Add melted shortening and stir to blend. Pour mixture into lightly-greased preheated cast-iron skillet and cook in a 425° oven for 20–25 minutes or until the top is golden brown. Serves 6.

Dorothy's Oat Bran Muffins

Personally, I'm opposed to the current health rage. Getting up early, jogging a couple of miles, and then breakfasting on something like oat bran is fine if you happen to be a racehorse. However, since most everybody seems inclined that way, we felt some sort of moral obligation to include an oat bran recipe. If you want an indication of how hard a good one is to find, we had to go all the way to Toronto to locate this one, and I must grudgingly admit that it is *good!* Thanks to Dorothy Wilson of Toronto, and occasionally the Texas Hill Country, for ending this search.

2 cups plain yogurt
2 tsp. soda
1 cup oatmeal
1 cup oat bran
2 cups flour
1 tsp. cinnamon

1 cup brown sugar, packed
2 eggs
2 tsp. baking powder
1/2 cup cooking oil
1 tsp. vanilla
1 cup raisins

Combine yogurt and soda in a non-reactive bowl. (This mixture will almost double in size, so plan your bowl accordingly.) Mix together oil, brown sugar, eggs, and vanilla. Add oat bran and oatmeal. Mix flour, cinnamon, and baking powder together. Add flour mixture alternately with yogurt mixture until well blended. Add raisins. Cook in greased muffin pans for 15–20 minutes in 375° oven. Makes 3 dozen.

Note: These freeze wonderfully. Just put 2 or 3 in a small freezer bag, take them out in the mornings and pop in the microwave. Or, if you don't have the space, halve the recipe.

Light Bread

Kneading dough is a wonderful way to get rid of tensions. There is a tremendous sense of satisfaction when you feel the texture change in the dough and when it is giving off that wonderful smell baking in the oven. And boy, does it taste good with homemade stews in the wintertime! Good toast? You bet!

2 pkgs. active dry yeast
About 1-1/2 cups warm water
1/4 cup sugar
3 Tbs. shortening

9–10 cups flour
Melted butter

Dissolve the yeast in 3/4 cup warm water. Add the remaining water (2–2/3 cups), salt, sugar, shortening, and about 4 cups flour. Beat until the mixture is smooth. Mix in enough of the remaining flour to make the dough easy to handle. Turn dough onto a lightly-floured surface and knead about 10 minutes. At this point the dough should have changed consistency and become elastic. If not, continue to knead. Place dough in a greased bowl, turn greased side up, and cover with a dish towel. Let it rise in a warm place until it is double in size. Punch the dough down and divide it into two pieces. Roll out each piece into a rectangle the width of your bread pan, roll up to form loaves, and place in a greased loaf pan. Brush the tops with melted butter. Recover and let it rise again until double. Cook in a 425° oven until deep brown and the loaves have a hollow sound when they are tapped. Makes two loaves.

Note: Rising time for bread depends upon the room temperature. It should take anywhere from 1 to 1–1/2 hours for each rising. Place your loaves of bread on the bottom rack in the oven so that the top of the loaf is in about the center of the oven. Use dark pans, not shiny ones, as they make a better crust. Remove loaves from pans immediately when they are done and cool them on a rack.

In photos at right we see the dough beginning its first rising (top), with first rising completed (center), and the finished product ready to cut and eat.

Chapter Five
The Thundering Herd
(When You've Decided to Go Beyond "Serves 8")

OK you're a hand in the kitchen. Everybody likes the goodies you cook. So, for whatever reason, you've committed to cater your first *big* event. You are about to find out why caterers charge so much.

First and foremost, adopt the KISS theory of management (Keep It Simple, Stupid!). KISS should become a "mantra." In line with that, never agree to do "sit-down dinners" for large groups. I can give you a long list of hotels that are completely equipped for banquets and they still can't get them right! Why do you think they call it the "rubber chicken circuit"?

Second, realize that the only way you're going to pull this off successfully is with thorough planning and organization. That means lots of lists and phone calls. Also, realize your limitations. I don't like to do barbecue dinners for more than a few hundred because of the size of my current pit. (That's not to say I couldn't come up with a larger pit in a heartbeat, if for instance, the White House should call.) Got to have your priorities!

—PLANNING AND MENUS—

As soon as possible, inspect the site of the event-to-be. Look for available power, lighting, serving facilities, kitchens (if any), dining areas, tables and chairs, vehicle access, water access, material handling equipment (if any), *waste* disposal, alcoholic beverage serving requirements, etc. All of these, and many more, go with the planning, menu selection, and actual execution of the event.

You should realize that you were selected for your cooking ability, not strength or artistic acclaim; therefore, inform the host and hostess that tables, chairs, tablecloths, and decorations aren't your bag and it's up to them to take care of that end. You've got enough to do, already. If they balk at this, either recommend a professional that you know can handle the job, or resign, shake hands, and have a farewell drink.

Plan your menu around:

1. The format—i.e., cocktail party, buffet dinner, open house, brunch, etc.
2. The budget—determine in real dollars what's available on a per-person basis. Do this even if you're doing your own personal event.
3. Recognize the menu limitations created by event site, equipment, etc.
4. Discard any recipe which requires close timing or minute individual attention. (See KISS above.)

To give you an example of how all these rules apply, we catered a wedding dinner several years ago where the entire event was outside in a cow pasture. No power (thankfully, it was in late afternoon), no running water, nothing but a bare patch of ground. As it was a "Texas-style" wedding, barbecue was the meat of choice. The briskets and ham went straight from the pit, uncarved, into a cooler to keep them warm and juicy. The 60-quart pot of beans (and its self-contained cooking unit) went into the pickup still bubbling, and the coleslaw and ice cream had been stashed earlier in a convenience store walk-in cooler. Upon our arrival we set up our tables, carved the meat, set out everything in their serving dishes, and were ready to serve an hour after arrival.

Lunch for a bunch . . . enough food for 100 hungry people.

If you've never done a large event before, do a "walk through" at home. Set up everything, sans food, but with serving equipment and utensils, just as you would want it. Then have a friend walk through the line. Make two lists. The first is what you have done. The second is the stuff you forgot to do. It's bad form to show up with a pot of soup and no bowls.

When planning your menu, first consider the theme, then your equipment and how you'd do it step-by-step. Try to select a combination of foods that can be done on/in the equipment you have on hand. Last year we catered a welcoming party with a German theme. The menu featured split pea soup, sausage, sauerkraut, dark bread, cold beer, and white wine. Once again, site amenities included very nice mesquite trees for shade and atmosphere . . . and nothing else. We cooked the soup in the big bean pot and served it bubbling. We combined the sausage and sauerkraut in stockpots and steamed them on a Coleman stove. Beer and wine were in the ice chests. Three pots, two heating units, 80 people served—no sweat!

COOKWARE AND EQUIPMENT

Go about adding to your equipment judiciously. It is quite easy to go crazy as a mad dog in a meathouse in a restaurant supply store—all those *goodies!* Equipment should be selected carefully. These are investments for the long term (and are usually priced accordingly). As a rule, you can scratch discount stores and department stores as a source of cookware although some department stores do carry good cutlery. Spend some time shopping restaurant supply stores, ask a few questions, and don't overlook the used equipment market.

If you haven't already got one, your first purchase should be a high quality, 10-inch chef's knife. Expect to pay $35–$75. You'll wonder how you ever lived without it. Treat it well and it'll be just as useful to your heirs. A slicing knife of the same size and quality is also necessary. See what I mean about prices? We'll assume that you have the required smaller knives or you wouldn't have read this far.

A large pot is next on the list. Assuming you have a 12 to 16-quart pot already (and lesser sizes, as well) something in the 40–60-quart size is the ticket. There are a variety of materials and they cost accordingly, the best (and dearest) being stainless steel with aluminum clad bottoms. Mine happens to be enamel-coated steel (about $200 cheaper). Although it's showing signs of wear now, it has lasted 12 years.

Serving equipment, bowls, steam trays, and utensils are the other staples. Fortunately, they are relatively inexpensive and can be bought on an "as needed" basis.

——— GETTING IT DONE ———

If you're doing this for an organization of which you're a member, recruit "grunt labor" from its ranks. Also, recruit a friend who is a knowledgeable cook to act as *sous*-chef. This is not the time for democracy. Autocracy is the only way to make this happen. Delegate clearly. The most frequently heard and hated words are, "But I thought you were bringing that!" *Everybody* has a list.

TIMING

Everything that can be prepared in advance and held, should be. Remember that the larger the cooking vessel, the longer it will take to come to a boil. The time can be reduced by using a larger heat source. You'll just have to experiment with your own combination. Once you've figured the required cooking time, add in prep time, transportation time, and set-up time. Then add in another hour just to be comfortable. Remember, if you cooked well, planned well, and packed well, the rest is but a walk in the park!

— SOME RECIPES FOR THE — THUNDERING HERD

Brisket

Usually brisket is the best choice for any size group over 12. You get the most meat per square inch of pit space. For two hundred people, I'll do eight briskets (as discussed elsewhere) and then 50 lbs. of sausage while the briskets are mellowing in the aluminum foil. Sausage takes about 2-1/2 hours to heat through and flavor at 200°. This mix gives 1/4 pound of beef and 1/4 pound of sausage per person. Some'll eat more, some less; it's a good average.

To complete this meal, figure 40 qts. of beans (20 lbs. dry) and 10 gallons of coleslaw—and don't forget 2 gallons of Ol' Red's Barbecue Sauce (do ahead), plus pickles, onions, jalapeños, bread, etc.

Chicken Hindquarters

On sale or not, as mentioned earlier, this is el cheapo. Figure 1-1/2 quarters per person. Guys will usually eat 2; ladies 1. For fifty people you'll need 6 ten-pound bags. Depending on size, there will be 12–16 quarters per bag, so you'll have a few extra. (The cook gets to eat!) Mix up a half gallon of seasoned oil and cook the hindquarters as directed elsewhere in this book. It takes two 2-1/2 hours session on my pit. Store the first batch in an aluminum-foil-lined cooler. When the second batch comes off, head for the event.

Hill Country Peach Sauce (3–4 recipes), Texas Vegetable Medley (6 recipes), and Fiesta Salad (4 recipes) round out the meal. Add drinks, garnishes, bread, etc. This is great in the summer. The Peach Sauce and Fiesta Salad are do-aheads and the Texas Medley is cooked on the spot in your 40–60-quart pot. Takes about an hour.

Fajitas

Fajitas require a sizeable pit that is portable (usually mutually exclusive terms). They are also labor intensive. Last fall I helped serve fajitas to over 300. There were 2 people cooking, 3 cutting, and 3 serving. If you happen to be one of the carvers, be prepared to stay bent over all through the meal! If you've got the pit space and help available, fajitas are great 'cause everything else—pico, guacamole, beans, etc., are all do-aheads. Forewarned is forearmed. Just figure 3 people to the pound of meat and adjust the recipe in "Stuff You Cook On A Pit" (Chapter One) for the number of folks at hand!

Chili

This is a prime choice for large groups. The recipe can be expanded for any size group. It's a meal in a bowl; the only limitation is the size of your pots. The only things extra are the garnishes and cold beer *(mandatory)*. Here's a good all-round recipe for up to 50 hungry folks, with seconds all around. Serve with sides of cheese, raw onion, jalapeños, and crackers.

> 25 lbs. meat, very lean, coarsely ground (1/2 inch at smallest)
> 10 onions, chopped and peeled
> 2-1/2 Tbs. garlic powder
> 1-1/2 cups dark chili powder
> 1/2 cup ground cumin
> 10 cans beef broth
> One 16-oz. can tomato sauce
> 20 fresh jalapeños, stems removed
> 2-1/2 Tbs. garlic powder
> 2 cups light chili powder
> 1/2 cup ground cumin
> 1-1/2 Tbs. cayenne
> 1-1/2 Tbs. white pepper
> 5 Tbs. MSG (optional)
> 3 Tbs. salt
> Two 16-oz. cans tomato sauce

Brown meat in batches. Use as many skillets as you have available burners. Drain meat and dump into your big pot. Add the next seven ingredients and water to cover. Bring to a boil and cook covered for 45 minutes, adding water as needed. Add everything else and cook for 45 additional minutes, adding water as needed. Stir frequently, or your chili will stick to the bottom. (A one-by-four works well for this.) Serves 50.

Beans for a Bunch

For the last 10 years a group of us have met for an old-fashioned, no rules, chili cook-off at a scenic site in the hills near Driftwood, Texas. Since we always meet on the last weekend in January, a big pot of beans with flour tortillas has always been the Friday night fare. I'll heat the tortillas on a large griddle warmed over the same burner that cooked the beans. (The griddle is actually a piece of 3/8-inch steel plate that was salvaged from a construction site—I swapped a 6-pack of beer for it!)

    20 lbs. dry pinto beans
    10 onions, peeled and quartered
    7–8 lbs. salt pork or 5–7 lbs. smoked shank ham (cut into
        chunks)
    One 12-oz. can jalapeños in *escabeche*
    3 Tbs. garlic powder
    3/4 cup chili powder
    1/4 cup cumin

In your big pot add beans and water to 3 inches of brim. Bring to a boil about an hour to an hour and a half. Turn off for two hours and allow beans to swell. Add everything else and boil gently for 4–6 hours or until beans are tender. Serves about 140–160.

Natha Caldwell with
60-quart portable
bean pot.

How To Cook A Pot Of Chili

1. Skin and dice nine (9) plump steers.
2. In a *very* large pot brown meat over high heat.
3. Add 1,600 onions (1 level pickup full) and 7,000 cloves of garlic, peeled and finely chopped.
4. Add 100 gallons of beef broth and 60 cases of Lone Star Beer.
5. Bring to a boil, reduce heat, and simmer for one hour.
6. Add 60 gallons tomato sauce and 200 pounds chili powder and other good things.
7. Simmer for one hour, add salt to taste, and serve with crackers.

Serves 20,000 (recipe may be doubled for large party)

This is what we distributed on March 1, 1986, at La Villita, San Antonio, when we cooked the world's largest pot of chili in celebration of Texas' 150th birthday party. It is basically the recipe we used, as the pot contained 4,000 pounds of meat that eventually turned into a pretty fair pot of chili. Amazingly, because the pot was so well built and heated it took only 6-1/2 hours from start to finish to cook the chili.

Chapter Six

Libations

L et us put to rest some foul rumors. Some shallow knaves have implied that I'll drink nearly anything that runs downhill. Not so! I don't drink buttermilk. On the other hand, a drink or two before dinner has much to recommend itself, and I concur.

Since most of our friends agree with this philosophy, many of the recipes are created for a group. The trick is to mix everything in a pitcher, leaving out the ice so that the drinks won't get watery.

A thought: We've found through trial and error that a white jug-wine, such as a Sauvigon Blanc, served ice cold, is an excellent complement to either piquant or smokey foods, such as Pasta Brasada, the Red Sauce for shrimp and oysters, or barbecued chicken. It has a round, quenching, fulfilling taste. These dishes are not ones that lend themselves to that dusty prize in your wine cellar, but to lusty young wines, meant to be quaffed copiously.

———— SUGGESTIONS FOR ———— BRUNCH

Bloody Mary

1-1/4 cups vodka
4 Tbs. Worchestershire sauce

10 dashes Tabasco sauce
Juice of 2-3 small limes
Salt, pepper, and celery salt to taste
Dash of garlic powder
Lime wedges
1 quart tomato juice

Mix all ingredients in a pitcher, pour into tall glasses that are filled with ice. Garnish with lime wedges. Serves 6.

English Mary

1-1/4 cups vodka or gin
2 Tbs. Worchestershire sauce
6 oz. canned beef broth
1-2 Tbs. horseradish
Juice of a lemon
24 oz. tomato juice
Salt and pepper to taste
1 light dash of onion powder (or more to taste)
Celery ribs

Combine everything but the celery in a pitcher, mixing well. Pour into tall glasses that are filled with ice. Garnish with celery ribs. Serves 6.

Bloody Maria

Here's the start for a brunch with a Mexican or Southwestern theme.

> 1 cup white tequila
> 32 oz. Snappy Tom tomato cocktail
> 2 fresh jalapeños, stemmed, seeded, and split lengthwise
>   into quarters
> Juice of 3 limes
> Salt and pepper to taste
> Thin slices of lime

Pour lime juice and tequila over jalapeños in a pitcher, and muddle the peppers to release their flavor. Add Snappy Tom, salt and pepper to taste. Pour into tall glasses which have been filled with ice. Float a lime slice on top of each glass. Serves 6.

Screwdriver

Ah! The breakfast of champions. Many a chili cook has started off a winning day with one of these.

> 1-1/4 cup vodka
> 1 quart orange juice (preferably fresh)
> Juice of 2 limes
> Lime wedges

Mix orange juice, vodka, and lime juice in a pitcher. Pour over ice in tall glasses. Add a lime wedge for garnish.

—— SUGGESTIONS FOR ——
PATIO SITTING

A Real Margarita

Countless hours and no small amount of loot have gone into a scientific study on this subject that has spanned decades. This is, as it should be, a true margarita—no sugar, no strawberries, and not frozen!

    1/2 Mexican lime
    3 oz. white tequila, Sauza or Jose Cuervo
    1 oz. Triple Sec or Cointreau

Into a cocktail shaker half filled with ice, squeeze the juice from the lime. Add tequila and Triple Sec. Shake vigorously to blend and chill. Strain into a chilled cocktail glass with a salted rim. Serves 1.

Green Monster

Be careful of this one—it's aptly named.

    2-3 oz. white tequila or rum or vodka
    2 small scoops lime sherbert
    Club soda

In a large festive glass, put two scoops lime sherbet and the liquor. Slowly add club soda to fill the glass. Sip through a straw. Serves 1.

Sangrita

When tequila, the "spirit" of Mexico, is on the menu, the traditional way to drink it is neat, with a chaser called *sangrita* (not to be confused with *sangria*, a wine-based drink). There are commercial versions available, but here's a homemade that is much tastier.

> 6 oz. tomato juice
> 3 oz. orange juice
> Juice of 1 to 2 limes
> Tabasco sauce to taste

Mix all ingredients together and serve 2–3 oz. as a chaser for each shot of tequila.

FINISHERS

Irish Coffee

> 1-1/2 oz. good Irish whiskey
> 1 Tbs. Creme de Cocoa
> 1 tsp. sugar
> Strong, hot, black coffee
> Whipped cream
> Nutmeg

Mix whiskey, cream de cacao, and sugar in the bottom of an Irish coffee mug. Fill with coffee to within 1/2 inch of top. Float whipped cream on top. Dust with nutmeg. Serves 1.

Spanish Coffee

1-1/2 oz. Kahlua
1 Tbs. Creme de Cacao
Strong, hot, black coffee
1 oz. heavy cream
Semi-sweet chocolate shavings

Mix Kahlua, Creme de Cacao, and coffee in a heavy mug. Stir in cream. Sprinkle chocolate shavings over each cup. Serves 1.

APPENDIX

——————— GLOSSARY———————

Ancho chili powder—A dark, full-bodied chili powder ground from the ancho chili, which is the dried form of the Poblano pepper.

Beef skirt—Long narrow strips of beef, cut from the "rib flap" area, customarily used for making fajitas.

Brisket—Large beef roast cut from the breast of the steer. Preferred cut of meat for many barbecuers.

Cascabel chili powder—*Hot* chili powder derived from the Cascabel peppers, a native of Mexico.

Chili pequins—Tiny peppers, roughly the size of raisins, quite hot with a lot of residual heat. (Residual heat stays with you for a long time.) Usually found dried. Native to south Texas and Mexico where they grow wild, they are now cultivated for the market.

Chine bone—On a rack of pork or lamb ribs, the longitudinal bone at the joining of ribs to spine. This should be removed prior to cooking to facilitate carving. Have your butcher do this!

Chipotle pepper—The jalapeño pepper that has been dried over mesquite smoke. A unique flavor enhancer without heat. Hard to find, but worth the hunt!

Chorizo—Very spicy Mexican sausage, readily available throughout the Southwest, and nationally in Hispanic markets.

Cumin (English) or *comino* (Spanish)—Either way it's a pungent spice common to Mexican and Southwestern cooking as well as Indian curries. Readily available everywhere.

Corn cobette—Sections of corn on the cob about 3 inches long, available frozen.

Escabeche—Seasoned oil used to preserve jalapeño and serrano peppers.

Feral hog—Wild hog of domestic origin found throughout the South.

Habanero sauce—The sauce made from a combination of habanero peppers and vinegar . . . *very hot.*

Half-and-half—Light cream; approximately 50% milk and 50% heavy cream.

Non-reactive container—Pans or bowls made out of glass, Corning Ware, stainless steel, or non-porous plastic. Cast iron and aluminum react chemically with acids found in citrus, tomatoes, pineapple, wine, vinegar, etc.

Packer trimmed—Refers to briskets as they are shipped from the meat packing plant, before the meat market butcher "pretties them up" for sale in the meat counter.

Poblano peppers—Large, mild, fleshy peppers. Often used to make chili rellenos (stuffed with cheese, then battered and fried). A staple ingredient in many Mexican dishes. The dried form is called *ancho* (see above).

Posole—White corn that has been treated with lye and dried. Also known as dry hominy, it is a staple of Southwestern cooking.

Ribeye, flap on — The whole uncut ribeye roast, bones removed, with the lower fat flap (or tail) intact.

Sauté—To brown quickly in a skillet with a mininal amount of cooking oil.

──── *SUPPLY SOURCES*────

Bolner's Fiesta Brand Products
426 Menchaca Street
San Antonio, TX 78207

Old Southwest Trading Company
P.O. Box 7545
Albuquerque, NM 87194

Pendery's Mexican Chile Supply
304 East Belknap Street
Ft. Worth, TX 76102

Santa Cruz Chili & Spice Co.
P.O. Box 177
Tumacacori, AZ 85640